Contents

Introduction

About Bullying is Volume 380 in the **issues** series. The aim of the series is to offer current, diverse information about important issues in our world, from a UK perspective.

ABOUT BULLYING

Recent studies show one in two people have experienced some form of bullying behaviour at some point in their life. Online bullying in particular has increased due to wider access to the internet and greater use of smartphones, social media and networking apps. This book looks at the latest UK statistics around bullying, its impact on victims and its prevalence in schools and workplaces alike.

OUR SOURCES

Titles in the **issues** series are designed to function as educational resource books, providing a balanced overview of a specific subject.

The information in our books is comprised of facts, articles and opinions from many different sources, including:

♦ Newspaper reports and opinion pieces

♦ Website factsheets

♦ Magazine and journal articles

♦ Statistics and surveys

♦ Government reports

♦ Literature from special interest groups.

A NOTE ON CRITICAL EVALUATION

Because the information reprinted here is from a number of different sources, readers should bear in mind the origin of the text and whether the source is likely to have a particular bias when presenting information (or when conducting their research). It is hoped that, as you read about the many aspects of the issues explored in this book, you will critically evaluate the information presented.

It is important that you decide whether you are being presented with facts or opinions. Does the writer give a biased or unbiased report? If an opinion is being expressed, do you agree with the writer? Is there potential bias to the 'facts' or statistics behind an article?

ASSIGNMENTS

In the back of this book, you will find a selection of assignments designed to help you engage with the articles you have been reading and to explore your own opinions. Some tasks will take longer than others and there is a mixture of design, writing and research-based activities that you can complete alone or in a group.

FURTHER RESEARCH

At the end of each article we have listed its source and a website that you can visit if you would like to conduct your own research. Please remember to critically evaluate any sources that you consult and consider whether the information you are viewing is accurate and unbiased.

Useful Websites

www.anti-bullyingalliance.org.uk

www.bulliesout.com

www.cambslearntogether.co.uk

www.campaignlive.co.uk

www.compassioninpolitics.com

www.ditchthelabel.org

www.independent.co.uk

www.inews.co.uk

www.journalistsresource.org

www.nationalbullyinghelpline.co.uk

www.ncb.org.uk

www.nhs.uk

www.ons.gov.uk

www.rcpath.org

www.respectme.org.uk

www.theconversation.com

www.theguardian.com

www.thiis.co.uk

www.wearencs.com

About Bullying

Editor: Tracy Biram

Volume 380

independence
educational publishers

First published by Independence Educational Publishers

The Studio, High Green

Great Shelford

Cambridge CB22 5EG

England

© Independence 2021

Copyright

Photocopy licence

ISBN-13: 978 1 86168 838 5

Printed in Great Britain

Zenith Print Group

Definition of bullying

Forms of bullying

Bullying behaviour across all types of bullying can represent itself in a number of different forms. Children and young people can be bullied in ways that are:

Physical – by being punched, pushed or hurt; made to give up money or belongings; having property, clothes or belongings damaged; being forced to do something they don't want to do.

Verbal – by being teased in a nasty way; called gay (whether or not it's true); insulted about their race, religion or culture; called names in other ways or having offensive comments directed at them.

Indirect – by having nasty stories told about them; being left out, ignored or excluded from groups.

Electronic / 'cyberbullying' – via text message; via instant messenger services and social network sites; via email; and via images or videos posted on the internet or spread via mobile phones.

Types of bullying

The term 'prejudice-related' bullying refers to a range of hurtful behaviour, physical or emotional or both, which causes someone to feel powerless, worthless, excluded or marginalised, and which is connected with prejudices around belonging, identity and equality in wider society – in particular, prejudices to do with:

♦ ethnic, cultural and religious backgrounds

♦ gender

♦ gender identity

♦ sexual identity

♦ special educational needs and disabilities

The Equality Act 2010 identifies nine 'protected characteristics' and children and young people can have or be perceived to have more than one 'protected characteristic' and as a result may be bullied because of a number of prejudices:

♦ age

♦ gender reassignment

♦ pregnancy and maternity

♦ religion or belief

♦ sexual orientation

♦ sex

♦ race

♦ marriage and civil partnership

♦ disability

2020

The above information is reprinted with kind permission from Cambridgeshire County Council ©2020 Cambs Learn Together

www.cambslearntogether.co.uk

Is banter bullying?

We all like a good lol. But does everyday banter ever become bullying? Is there a line and does it get crossed? NCS grads, Charlotte and Jazmyn, take on the debate.

By Jazmyn Elizabeth, Charlotte Symons and NCS (National Citizen Service)

Jazmyn: Banter is not bullying

'Banter' is a modern term that has grown popular over the last few years, usually in reference to the act of mocking or disparaging a friend, sometimes an acquaintance.

One might argue that what may be harmless to one may be hurtful to another.

However, I'm of the opinion that as a generation we are becoming too sensitive. We shut down anyone with differing opinions to us; we are labelled as bigots if we have a tougher political stance; we are frowned upon for making controversial jokes, or black comedy. And now we can't even tease people?

The truth is, while at a glance jocular insults at another's expense may seem mean, they actually do something really special. They stop us from taking ourselves too seriously and allow us to turn something negative into a source of comedy. They make people laugh, and there can never be enough laughter in the world.

Camaraderie is an important part of youth, and 'banter' is an even playing field – you are not being targeted in quite the same way. Bullying is repetitively attacking someone with malicious intent, while banter teaches us how to deal with our differences and not to be vain.

If you're sensitive about something, finding humour in whatever worries you, can help you become resilient, even immune. It can build backbone and wit, equipping us with the ability to shrug things off. So when somebody genuinely insults you, it won't faze you. Your weak spots are not weak if you accept them, share them with others and make light of them together.

Charlotte: Banter is bullying

Everyone's used a good bit of banter at some point in their life, whether joking around with friends and family, or using humour in a sentence to make the person you're talking to laugh. Even memes include banter. However, is it really that positive? Is banter something we should be careful of? Here are my thoughts.

As I've gotten older and reached my late teens, I've heard banter being used in a variety of ways, even more so as the people and friends around me have grown up into teenagers, college students and uni students too. Banter seems to be used a lot more often than not these days, but I don't think that this is worth celebrating. In fact, in my opinion, banter is a form of bullying. I hear you asking why? Why should a joke be counted as bullying? Well, let me tell you.

I've been a college student for over a year now, so I've definitely heard my fair share of banter being thrown around and people insulting others and saying it's "just banter". Here's the issue; not only am I hearing this in college, but outside of it too, around my local area and even in surrounding towns. People will use banter as an excuse to hurt someone else's feelings. Whilst some may say that the receiving person is a little too sensitive, or that they need to lighten up and stop being melancholy, I disagree.

In our society, there's too much negativity. Instead of poking fun at others and insulting them using banter, we should be spreading light and laughter! We should use positive comments and respect those we meet. You won't ever know how people really feel about themselves, and although you might just label what you're saying as banter, a laugh, or a joke, you may be targeting someone's deepest insecurities, and hurting them with a 'harmless' joke.

Banter is supposed to be fun and make you laugh, but it can also just be a way to make people numb to negativity and that's not how playful jokes with friends should shape you as a person. Words that cause pain can be something you never forget, and this is why I feel that banter is bullying.

11 November 2019

www.wearencs.com

Baiting

What is baiting?

The dictionary describes to 'bait' someone as:

'To intentionally make a person angry by saying or doing things to annoy them'

For example:

♦ Ignore him - he's just baiting you.

♦ I suspect he was just baiting me.

Others describe baiting as:

A provocative act used to solicit an angry, aggressive or emotional response from another individual

Baiting and bullying

Baiting can be used in bullying both on and offline. It can be used to bully someone to get 'a rise' out of them and it can be used to antagonise those who might be bullying others to get them to bully. Sometimes baiting is used secretively to try and get a person to explode in a rage or react negatively/loudly so that they get into trouble.

What NOT to do:

♦ Don't take the bait!

♦ Don't argue with a person or appeal to their sense of reason or logic while they are baiting you. They want you to rise to it!

♦ Don't retaliate and fall into a trap.

What TO do:

♦ Learn to recognise baiting for what it is. If you know what they are trying to do it is easier to relationalise it.

♦ Remember that the bait you can see often has nothing to do with what the other person really wants.

♦ Remember that what the person is feeling is temporary and they will probably feel different in a few days or a few hours.

♦ Talk to an adult you trust such as a teacher or parent and explain what they are doing and why you think they are doing it.

♦ If falsely accused, politely, briefly and calmly state the truth one time only.

♦ Try to remove yourself from the situation calmly. End the conversation and exit the space/room.

♦ Get support - describe what has happened to someone who understands your situation and can help you come up with a reasoned, effective plan of how to deal with it.

Remember, bullying is NOT your fault.

03 Aug 2017

Prejudice-based bullying

Bullying behaviour may be a result of prejudice that relates to perceived or actual differences.

Bullying behaviour may be a result of prejudice that relates to perceived or actual differences. This can lead to prejudice and discriminatory language or behaviour, including racism, sexism, homophobia, biphobia or transphobia.

Respect for All states:

'Prejudice-based bullying is when bullying behaviour is motivated by prejudice based on an individual's actual or perceived identity; it can be based on characteristics unique to a child or young person's identity or circumstance.'

According to research, anti-bullying work which clearly addresses the particular needs of vulnerable or minority groups is more effective. In order to respond effectively to incidents as they arise, we must also address the root cause of prejudice.

To address the years of unfavourable treatment experienced by some groups, The Equality Act 2010 makes it unlawful to discriminate against people with a 'protected characteristic'. These are:

- Age
- Disability
- Gender reassignment
- Pregnancy and maternity
- Marriage and civil partnership
- Race
- Sex
- Religion or belief
- Sexual orientation

Prejudice can lead to bullying for a variety of reasons...

Prejudice-based bullying includes the protected characteristics, but prejudice can and does extend beyond these and can lead to bullying for many other reasons.

Additional support needs can arise for any reason for any length of time. Additional support may be required to overcome needs arising from learning environment; health or disability; family circumstances or social and emotional factors. A child or young person may be bullied because they have an additional support need and, crucially, being bullied can also lead to an additional support need.

Age: Although prejudice and discrimination based on age is not applicable in school settings, it can affect children and young people in settings such as the workplace, in further and higher education, and in wider society.

Asylum Seekers and Refugees: Stigma, caused by a lack of knowledge and understanding of asylum seekers and refugees, can mean children with this status may be at greater risk of being bullied. In addition, reluctance to burden parents or carers with extra worries can allow bullying to go undetected and continue.

Body image and physical appearance can be hugely important to children and young people, with bullying because of body image having the potential to negatively impact upon their wellbeing.

Disablist bullying: People who bully others may see children and young people with disabilities as being less able to defend themselves and/or tell an adult what has happened. The bullying behaviour is likely to be focused upon their specific disability or disabilities, whether they are in mainstream schooling or in specialist provision.

Gypsy/Travellers: This group of children and young people are a particularly discriminated against and marginalised group, and concerns about bullying are especially acute for secondary schools. Perceived risks about bullying and parents' own experiences of discriminatory behaviour may lead to low levels of enrolment and poor attendance for Gypsy/Traveller children and young people, as well as early exit from formal education. Other Traveller families, such as Roma, may have similar concerns.

Sexual orientation & homophobic bullying: Bullying based on sexual orientation is motivated by a prejudice against lesbian, gay or bisexual (LGB) people. It is also commonly referred to as 'homophobic bullying' but can also be expanded to recognise the specific experiences of bisexual young people using the term 'biphobic bullying'. Children and young people do not necessarily have to be gay, lesbian or bisexual themselves to experience 'homophobic bullying'. This type of bullying may be directed towards young people perceived to be LGB; those that do not conform to gender norms; and those who have gay friends or family. Although homophobic bullying is distinct from sexist and transphobic bullying, it is related to these forms of bullying through underlying sexist attitudes.

Intersectionality: It's important to understand the different and unequal social and economic outcomes for particular groups, based on interactions between race, class, gender, sexual orientation, disability, age and ethnicity. In the context of anti-bullying, we must consider people's experiences of belonging to one or more of these groups, people's prejudice towards them and how this can lead to inequality in attainment and wellbeing.

Care Experienced children and young people: are vulnerable to bullying behaviour for a number of reasons, such as regular changes in schools or where they are placed. Forming relationships with peers and adults can be made even more difficult due to early childhood adversity.

Marriage/Civil Partnership: Whilst it is unlikely that a school-aged pupil will experience direct prejudice and discrimination as a result of being in a same sex marriage or civil partnership, there could be instances of indirect discrimination if they are associated with someone who is. This type of discrimination can also affect children and young people in other settings, such as workplaces, further and higher education and in wider society.

Racial bullying: Children and young people from minority ethnic groups often experience bullying based on perceived differences in dress, communication, appearance, beliefs and/or culture as well as their skin colour and accent. The status of the ethnic group a child belongs to (or people assume they belong to) can often lead to a child or young person experiencing bullying behaviour. This can arise from a misguided and/or learned belief that they are less valued and 'deserve' to be treated differently, or with less respect.

Religion and belief: Lack of knowledge and understanding about the traditions, beliefs and etiquette of different faiths can lead to religious intolerance. Lack of awareness about the differences in practices of religions such as prayer times, dietary requirements, fasting and the wearing of religious clothing or articles of faith can result in misunderstandings and stereotyping, which may lead to bullying. People who have no religion or belief are also protected under the Equality Act.

Sectarianism: Most people understandably associate Sectarianism with religion, however, the reality of prejudice means that your family background, the football team you support, the community you live in, the school you attend and even the colour of your clothing can mark you out for sectarian abuse - whatever your beliefs may be. In Scotland, sectarianism is most often related to Protestant and Roman Catholic divisions within Christianity but can also relate to other religions, such as Sunni and Shia Muslims within Islam, and Orthodox and Reform Jews within Judaism.

Sexism and gender: Bullying in the form of derogatory language and the spreading of malicious rumours can be used to regulate both girls' and boys' behaviour. These terms can be of an explicit sexual nature and it is worth noting that many can involve the use of terms for people who are gay and lesbian as a negative towards a person's masculinity or femininity. Sexism and gender stereotypes feed into homophobia, biphobia and transphobia. Gender stereotyping, based on the notion of acceptable and unacceptable male and female behaviour, can leave children and young people who are not perceived to conform to these notions vulnerable to indirect and direct bullying.

Gender identity and transphobic bullying: The term 'transgender' is an umbrella-term for those whose 'gender identity' or expression differs in some way from the gender assigned to them at birth. Gender identity reflects an individual's internal sense of self as being male, female, or an identity between or outside the two. Transgender people face significant societal prejudice, largely because they are perceived as not conforming to gender stereotypes, expectations and norms. As a result, transgender or gender 'variant' children and young people can be particularly vulnerable to bullying, such as transphobic and homophobic name calling or deliberately mis-gendering them. An individual may also experience transphobic bullying as a result of a perception that a parent, relative or other significant figure is transgender.

Young Carers: The lives of young carers can be significantly affected by their responsibility to care for a family member who has a physical illness or disability, mental health problem, sensory or learning disability or issues with the misuse of drugs or alcohol. Young carers are at risk of bullying for a variety of reasons. Depending on responsibilities at home, they may find themselves being unable to fully participate in school or after-school activities or 'fun stuff'. This can make it difficult for them to form relationships; it can hinder successful transitions or lead to educational difficulties.

Socio-economic prejudice: Bullying due to socio-economic status can take place in any community. Small differences in perceived family income, living arrangements, social circumstances or values can be used as a basis for bullying

behaviours. These behaviours, such as mocking speech patterns, accents, belongings, clothing, etc, can become widespread through those considering themselves to be in the dominant social economic group.

Bullying of children who endure parental substance misuse can also be prevalent.

Hate crime

Hate crime is defined through the law as a crime motivated by malice or ill-will towards individuals because of their actual or perceived disability, race, religion, sexual orientation or transgender identity. A hate crime can take a number of forms that are potentially criminal and should be treated as such. Adults, children and young people can seek appropriate advice and guidance from Police Scotland if they feel a hate crime may have taken place. There is no legal definition of bullying in Scotland and as such bullying is not a crime. Bullying can be motivated by prejudice similar to hate crime, but the difference is when a crime has taken place, such as assault, graffiti or a breach of the peace which has been motivated by prejudice. The decision to proceed will rest with the Procurator Fiscal's Office. The presumption should be against criminalising children and young people wherever possible unless it is in the public interest.

Equality, equity & diversity

Equality is more than simply treating everyone the same. Not everyone needs exactly the same treatment because we are not all starting from the same place with the same privilege and support. Some people, and some groups of people, have and still do experience less favourable treatment than others. Promoting equality is about challenging inequality. It means challenging language and behaviours that lead to people being treated less favourably, or having poorer outcomes at school or in life.

Equity is about addressing the imbalance and making sure those who need more help, support or protection can get it. It is not enough to simply give everyone the same resources or tools to succeed, people may need tools or resources specific to their circumstances. This might mean taking steps to help those with less money get to school or college, or making sure those with a disability can enjoy the same places and experiences as everyone else.

Diversity aims to recognise, respect and value people's differences. Diversity doesn't just tolerate difference, it acknowledges and celebrates the richness it can bring. **Fully integrating and embedding equity, equality and diversity into an organisation relies on a culture where language and behaviour is challenged. When we work with or have children, we must create environments where difference is celebrated and prejudice is challenged.**

September 2020

Bullying experiences

Statistics from Part 1 of Ditch The Label's *Annual Bullying Survey 2020,* drawing on the experiences of 13,387 people aged 12–18 in the UK.

Being bullied - perceived motives

From those who have been bullied within the last 12 months: **Why do you think you were bullied?**

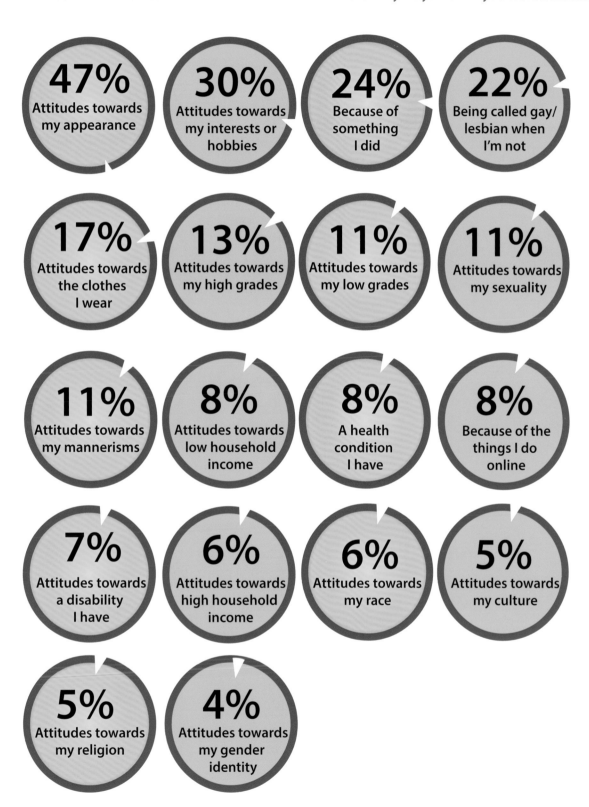

47% Attitudes towards my appearance

30% Attitudes towards my interests or hobbies

24% Because of something I did

22% Being called gay/lesbian when I'm not

17% Attitudes towards the clothes I wear

13% Attitudes towards my high grades

11% Attitudes towards my low grades

11% Attitudes towards my sexuality

11% Attitudes towards my mannerisms

8% Attitudes towards low household income

8% A health condition I have

8% Because of the things I do online

7% Attitudes towards a disability I have

6% Attitudes towards high household income

6% Attitudes towards my race

5% Attitudes towards my culture

5% Attitudes towards my religion

4% Attitudes towards my gender identity

Being bullied - impact

From those who have been bullied within the last 12 months: **How did it impact you?**

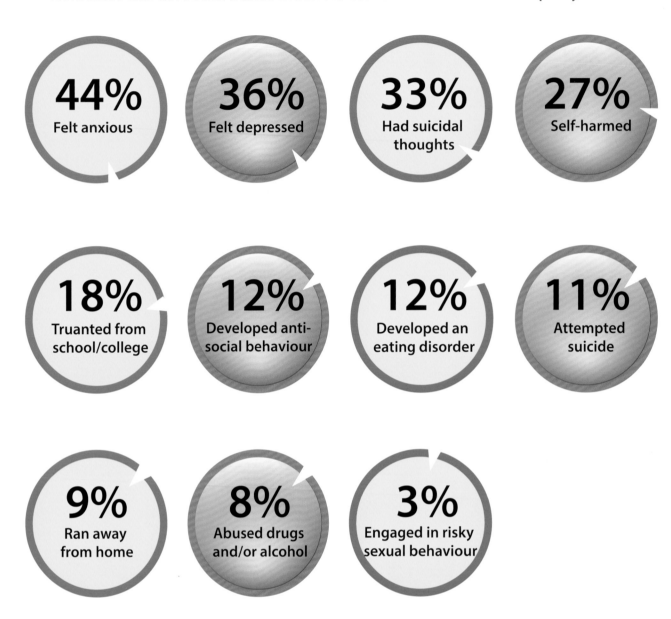

44% Felt anxious

36% Felt depressed

33% Had suicidal thoughts

27% Self-harmed

18% Truanted from school/college

12% Developed anti-social behaviour

12% Developed an eating disorder

11% Attempted suicide

9% Ran away from home

8% Abused drugs and/or alcohol

3% Engaged in risky sexual behaviour

Being bullied - other responses

From those who have been bullied within the last 12 months:

Do you think you deserved to be bullied?

10% said yes

23% were unsure

67% said no

What did you do when someone did bully you?

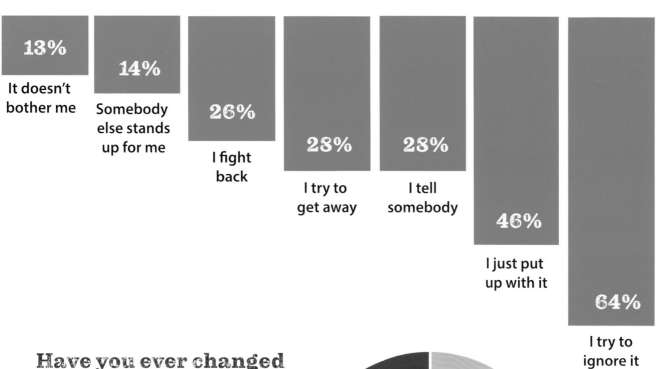

13% It doesn't bother me

14% Somebody else stands up for me

26% I fight back

28% I try to get away

28% I tell somebody

46% I just put up with it

64% I try to ignore it

Have you ever changed or hidden part of who you are in order to avoid getting bullied from other people?

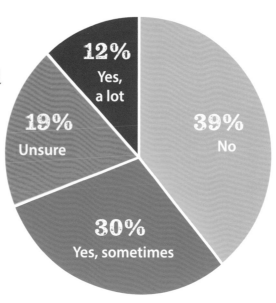

12% Yes, a lot

19% Unsure

39% No

30% Yes, sometimes

Moral compass

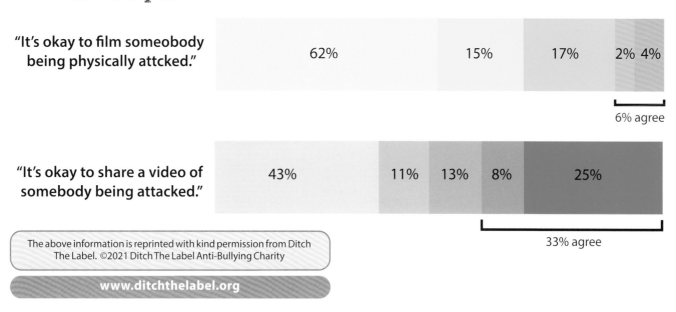

"It's okay to film someobody being physically attcked."

62% 15% 17% 2% 4%

6% agree

"It's okay to share a video of somebody being attacked."

43% 11% 13% 8% 25%

33% agree

Online bullying in England and Wales: year ending March 2020

Estimates of the prevalence and nature of online bullying among children using data from the 10–15 year olds' Crime Survey for England and Wales (CSEW).

Main points

♦ There is no legal definition of bullying, but it is often described as behaviour that hurts someone else, physically or emotionally, and can happen anywhere - at school, at home or online.

♦ Around one in five children aged 10 to 15 years in England and Wales (19%) experienced at least one type of online bullying behaviour in the year ending March 2020, equivalent to 764,000 children.

♦ More than half (52%) of those children who experienced online bullying behaviours said they would not describe these behaviours as bullying, and one in four (26%) did not report their experiences to anyone.

♦ Being called names, sworn at or insulted and having nasty messages about them sent to them were the two most common online bullying behaviour types, experienced by 10% of all children aged 10 to 15 years.

♦ Nearly three out of four children (72%) who had experienced an online bullying behaviour experienced at least some of it at school or during school time.

Statistician's comments

"Greater use of smartphones, social media and networking applications means online bullying can follow a child anywhere they go. Using new data from the crime survey we can see that around 1 in 5 children between the ages of 10 to 15 had experienced some form of online bullying in the previous 12 months.

"This compares with 2 in 5 children who experienced bullying in person, and whilst these data were collected before the coronavirus pandemic, children's isolation at home and increased time spent on the internet is likely to have had a substantial impact on the split between real world and cyber bullying."

–Sophie Sanders from the Office for National Statistics Centre for Crime and Justice.

Notes: Main points. In the survey, children were first asked to identify any nasty things that had happened to them or been done to them from a list of behaviours commonly recognised as bullying. Children were later separately asked whether or not they would describe their experiences mentioned as "bullying".

Prevalence of bullying

In the year ending March 2020, an estimated one out of five children aged 10 to 15 years in England and Wales experienced at least one type of online bullying behaviour (19%). This equates to approximately 764,000 children.

Online bullying has been increasingly enabled by wider access to the internet and greater use of smartphones, social media and networking applications. By comparison, twice as many children (38%) reported that they had experienced a bullying behaviour in person. A smaller percentage experienced a bullying behaviour by a telephone or mobile phone call (4%). As some children experienced multiple types of bullying behaviour, overall 42% of children aged 10 to 15 years experienced some form of bullying behaviour in the year ending March 2020.

There was no significant difference in the proportion of girls (20%) and boys (17%) who had experienced an online bullying behaviour. However, the prevalence of online bullying was significantly higher for children with a long-term illness or disability (26%) than those without (18%). Asian or Asian British children were also significantly less likely to have experienced an online bullying behaviour (6%) than White children (21%), Black or Black British children (18%) and Mixed Ethnic group children (19%).

As the data used for this publication relate to the period prior to the coronavirus (COVID-19) pandemic and lockdown, with children's isolation at home and increased time spent on the internet, the split between in person and online bullying is likely to have changed substantially during this period.

Out of all children who had experienced a form of online bullying behaviour, slightly less than half (48%) stated that they had experienced two or more types of online bullying behaviours.

The number of times online bullying behaviours were experienced varied between different types. Being called names, sworn at and insulted was the most frequently experienced online bullying behaviour, with 20% of children who experienced this type of behaviour stating they experienced it every day or a few times a week. An additional 20% of children experienced it once or twice a week.

Experiencing bullying behaviours through being sent messages, images or videos was the method with the highest percentage across all types of online bullying behaviours. Other methods of carrying out online bullying behaviours included posting online messages, images or videos about children, contacting children in a chatroom, and through online games. The percentages for these methods varied for each type of online bullying behaviour.

Prevalence of bullying

Almost one in five children experienced at least one type of online bullying behaviour in the previous 12 months

Proportion of children aged 10 to 15 years who experienced online bullying behaviours in the previous 12 months by type of bullying behaviour, England and Wales, year ending March 2020

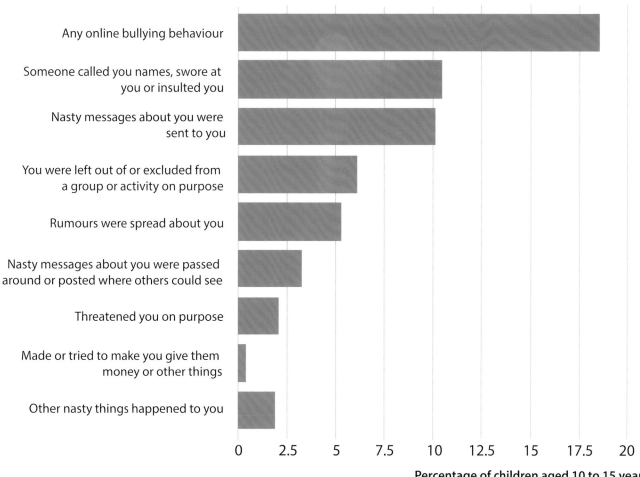

Percentage of children aged 10 to 15 years

Source: Office for National Statistics - Crime Survey for England and Wales

Children who experienced an online bullying behaviour through messages being sent to them, posted online or in chatrooms were asked whether these were private messages to them, group messages or something that anyone could see online.

Private messages were used more frequently for types of bullying that do not necessarily involve any other children except the victim, such as someone calling them names, swearing at them or insulting them and nasty messages about them being sent to them.

As online bullying behaviours by private messages are only experienced by the victim, it is more likely that they will go unnoticed unless someone is told.

Group messages were more frequently used for types of online bullying behaviour that mainly involve other people such as nasty messages about children being passed around or posted where others could see and children being left out of or excluded from a group or activity on purpose.

Children were also asked whether the online bullying behaviours that they experienced were carried out by the same person or same group of people. Slightly over half of the children (51%) answered that the online bullying behaviours they experienced were carried out by the same people. Just over a third (36%) answered that they were not carried out by the same people, while 13% did not know.

Bullying and school

School has a central role in bullying. It is the place where children spend a lot of their time daily and interact with other children who may display bullying behaviours. It can be a place where bullying takes place but also a place where children may seek direct help from their teachers or school staff.

In the year ending March 2020, 7 out of 10 (70%) children aged 10 to 15 years who experienced an online bullying behaviour said this was by someone from their school.

Another important finding concerning schools is children's perception of how well their school deals with bullying. More than two-thirds of children (68%) believed that their school deals with bullying very well or quite well, while a quarter (25%) believed that their school does not deal with bullying very well or not at all well. A minority (6%) answered that bullying is not a problem at their schools.

These figures varied depending on whether children experienced at least one online bullying behaviour in the previous year. For children who had experienced online bullying, the percentage saying that their school does not deal with bullying very well or not well at all was more than double (44%) that for children who had not (21%).

Perception and impact of online bullying

Around 7 out of 10 children were emotionally affected by the online bullying behaviours experienced.

Bullying, among other factors, can have an impact on a child's emotional well-being. For the year ending March 2020, 22% of children aged 10 to 15 years who had experienced a type of online bullying behaviour said that they were emotionally affected a lot by these incidents. A further 47% said that they were a little affected and 32% said that they were not affected at all. This means that almost 7 out of 10 children

(68%) were emotionally affected to an extent by the online bullying behaviours experienced.

An estimated one in three children (32%) who experienced online bullying behaviours reported it to their teachers, and 18% reported it to another member of staff. However, children most commonly reported their online bullying experiences to parents (56%), while 19% reported it to other family members. Helplines were used by 1% of children to report online bullying behaviours they had experienced, while 15% of children reported these experiences to someone else.

Slightly over one in four children (26%) did not report their online bullying experiences. There is a significant difference between boys and girls, with 34% of boys not reporting these experiences to anyone compared with 15% of girls.

An estimated 52% of children said they would not describe the online bullying behaviours they experienced as bullying.

Nature of online bullying

Being called names, sworn at and insulted was the most frequently experienced online bullying behaviour.

Frequency of online bullying behaviours experienced by children aged 10 to 15 years in the prevous 12 months, by type of bullying behaviour, England and Wales, year ending March 2020

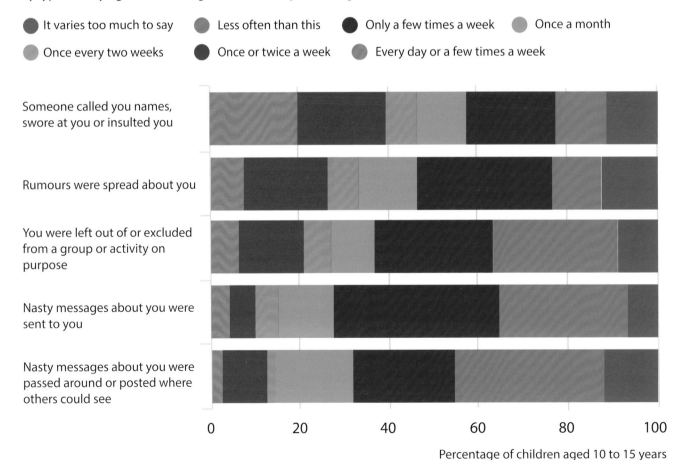

- It varies too much to say
- Less often than this
- Only a few times a week
- Once a month
- Once every two weeks
- Once or twice a week
- Every day or a few times a week

Percentage of children aged 10 to 15 years

Source: Office for National Statistics – Crime Survey for England and Wales
Notes: Types of online bullying behaviour with an unweighted base of less than 50 were excluded from this figure

The most common reason for not reporting experiences of online bullying behaviours to anyone was that the victim did not think it was important

Reasons for children aged 10 to 15 years not reporting online bullying behaviours experienced in the previous 12 months, England and Wales, year ending March 2020

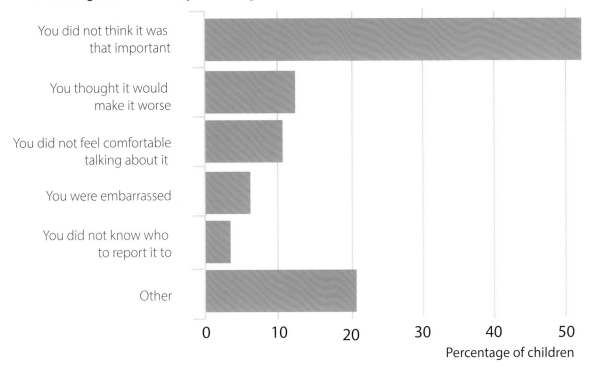

Percentage of children

Source: Office for National Statistics – Crime Survey for England and Wales
Notes: Percentages may not sum up to 100 as respondents may have given more than one answer

There is no legal definition of bullying, but it is often described as behaviour that hurts someone else, physically or emotionally, and can happen anywhere – at school, at home or online. Because there is no single definition, bullying can be perceived differently by individuals, particularly between adults and children, and this can depend on the context in which something is taking place and who it is carried out by.

In the survey, children were first asked to identify any nasty things that had happened to them or been done to them from a list of behaviours commonly recognised as bullying. Children were later separately asked whether or not they would describe their experiences mentioned as "bullying".

More than half of the children (52%) who experienced an online bullying behaviour answered that they would not describe their experiences as bullying, while 29% did describe their experiences as bullying and 19% did not know. This could be for a number of reasons including the child was not aware these behaviours are commonly recognised as bullying, they did not consider the incident to be significant or they did not want to admit that they had been bullied.

There is a clear relationship between the emotional impact of online bullying behaviours, whether children would describe it as bullying and whether they report it.

Children who said they were affected a lot were more likely to report their experiences with 9% not reporting these to anyone compared with 20% of children who were affected a little and 42% of children who were not affected at all.

Children who described their experiences of online bullying behaviours as bullying were also significantly more likely to have reported these to someone. Of those children who described their experiences as bullying, almost three out of four children (74%) reported their experiences to their parents or guardian, and 53% reported them to their teachers. In comparison, of the children that did not describe their experiences as bullying, 40% reported their experiences to their parent or guardian and 17% reported them to their teacher. An estimated 35% of children who did not describe these behaviours as bullying did not report them to anyone, compared with 11% of children who did.

Out of the children who said their experiences of online bullying behaviours affected them a lot, 58% described their experiences as bullying. In comparison, 30% of children who were affected a little and 10% of children who were not emotionally affected at all by their experiences described them as bullying.

Notes: Perception and impact of online bullying
Percentages may not sum up to 100% as children may have given more than one answer.

16 November 2020

Friendships help, say children – as one in three report being bullied since Covid outbreak

Bullying is still a significant problem in children's lives, with a third (33.5%) of children in England saying they've been victims during the last six months. A poll of 2,000 11 to 16-year-olds, published to mark Anti-Bullying Week, found that one in five children said they were on the receiving end of bullying behaviour once per week or more.

However, the poll, commissioned by the Anti-Bullying Alliance, suggests that Covid-19 has affected how bullying takes place, with rising numbers of children reporting incidents online or in their communities compared to a similar survey last year, and fewer children saying they had been bullied in school.

Of those who reported being bullied recently, 38% said it had taken place online, a rise from 29% in a pre-Covid survey conducted in 2019. There was a similar rise in reports of bullying in the community: with 16% of children who experienced bullying saying it had happened in their community, compared to 9% last year.

At the same time, the lengthy closure of schools for most children seems likely to account for a drop in bullying in school settings, with 74% of young people who reported being bullied in 2020 saying it took place in school, a fall from 83% in 2019.

The majority of children (65%) stressed that having lots of good friends helped protect them from being bullied. However, the number of children reporting they had more than one good friend fell by 4 percentage points, from 91% before coronavirus to 86.5% in October 2020.

Many children (38%) were anxious about returning to school in September because they feared suffering bullying behaviour. Of those who had been bullied recently, alongside the three-quarters who said it took place within school, 26% said the journey to and from school was a flashpoint.

On a positive note, an overwhelming majority (80%) said that if we work together, we can unite to reduce bullying. This message will be highlighted in the three-quarters of schools in England expected to celebrate Anti-Bullying Week this year - reaching over 7 million children and drawing on teaching resources made possible with support from SafeToNet.

Odd Socks Day for Anti-Bullying Week takes place on the Monday 16th Nov, when CBeebies and CBBC star Andy Day and his band Andy and the Odd Socks will be launching their new charity single 'The Kids Are United'.

The song's video, made by hundreds of pupils in their 'bubbles' in schools across the country, encourages young and old alike to wear odd socks to school or work and celebrate what makes us all unique. The video features 11-year-old dance sensation, Princess K, sharing fresh dance moves in support of Anti-Bullying Week, as well as Libera boys choir, a hugely popular and internationally renowned choir from South London. Andy and the band will be sharing their song and discussing bullying in an online assembly to schools across the country on the morning of Odd Socks Day, which also features messages of support from Mo Farah, McFly and Anne-Marie.

Quotes from young people taking part in the poll:

♦ "I enjoyed being at home so no one could bully me."

♦ "Some children might not have been able to see their friends for a lot of months while the coronavirus lockdown was going on."

♦ "The more isolated kids risk to be bullied more now."

♦ "Think lots of friendships have been lost."

♦ "People cough and they say 'you have the rona.'"

♦ "Seen my Chinese friend being bullied because of the virus."

Martha Evans, Director of the Anti-Bullying Alliance, said:

"It's clear that bullying remains a significant problem for many children across the country, and we know that these experiences can have a lasting impact well into adulthood. But this year we have witnessed the power that people can have when they unite to tackle a common challenge. If we are serious about reducing bullying, we have to harness that energy and work together. Be it online, in the community or in school, we

all have a part to play and it's time we came together, friends and family, classmates and colleagues, and unite against bullying."

Andy Day, CBeebies and CBBC star and lead singer of Andy and the Odd Socks, said:

"Because of the pandemic, kids have missed out on so many of the things that they love. Each and every child will have a story to tell about the different ways it has affected them. Now they are back at school, we are all responsible for equipping children with the simple message that we are all different, and that's a good thing! To bring the message home, we've recorded a brilliant new charity song and video especially for Anti-Bullying Week called 'The Kids Are United'. We spoke to school children all over the country to help write the rap and we hope it inspires everyone to get involved or at the very least to get up and dance!"

Children and Families Minister Vicky Ford said:

"Bullying is never acceptable in any form, and we must all take a stand against bullying to create a safe place for children in the classroom and online. Throughout the pandemic we have worked with organisations who are supporting schools in their efforts to tackle bullying.

"The introduction of relationships education will teach pupils how to treat others with respect and where to get help if they are suffering bullying online or face-to-face. We are also bringing in legislation that protects against harmful behaviour online, which is especially important as we all spend more time online, working or socialising virtually."

18 November 2020

Income inequality and bullying linked in new study

By Clarke Merrefield

Growing up in a country with wide income inequality is associated with being bullied during early adolescence, according to a new paper in JAMA Pediatrics from nine researchers representing universities around the world.

The authors analyzed survey responses from 874,203 kids aged 11 to 15 across 40 countries, mostly in Europe and North America. They found the strongest association between these experiences:

♦ Living from birth to 4 in areas with high income inequality.

♦ Being bullied at school.

Put another way, there is a link between early-life inequality and being bullied at school later in life.

"Being a developmental psychologist, I'm interested in the early life effects — when does this [association] get under the skin?" says lead author Frank Elgar, a researcher at McGill University in Montreal. "Here, the most consequential exposure is infancy."

What's happening is unclear, but it's happening before kids start going to school

The team from universities in Canada, Israel, the Netherlands, Poland and Ireland pooled data from 1994 to 2014 from the World Health Organization's Health Behavior in School-Aged Children, a cross-national survey conducted every four years.

The data span time and geography, but the survey doesn't intentionally re-survey the same children across years. It provides a snapshot every four years of key health indicators among children aged 11 to 15.

Some countries did not participate in every survey. The U.S. did not participate in 1994 and 2014.

"There were interruptions, [countries] dropped out due to financial reasons," Elgar says.

Given the sheer number of survey participants, Elgar is confident in the association between early exposure to income inequality and being bullied later in life. But the strength of the association is unclear.

"The associations we found are consistent and reinforce the literature showing that income inequality is related to interpersonal violence and various measures of decreased social capital," Elgar says.

Anti-bullying efforts at schools are important for reducing bullying, according to the authors, but these results indicate that schools can't do everything. What's happening at home also matters.

"That the effect is there before they reach school age suggests it's not an outcome, not a product of school resources or programming," Elgar says.

Walk, don't run with these results

The number of survey participants is massive and the authors control for several variables — changes in inequality from birth to when bullying was captured, national per capita income, family socioeconomic position, and birth year — but they couldn't control for everything.

"Kids in more unequal settings probably had a range of other factors that we can't control for," Elgar says.

The WHO data define bullying in broad strokes, with questions adapted from the 40-question Olweus Bully-Victim Questionnaire. Questions included:

♦ How often have you been bullied at school during the past couple of months?

♦ How often have you taken part in bullying other students during the past couple of months?

The authors did not associate early-life inequality and being a bully, a result they call "unexpected." The reason may have to do with self-reporting. The questionnaire is better at capturing results about being bullied than bullying, according to the authors.

In other words, kids seem to be more forthcoming when they're being bullied than when they're doing the bullying. This work appears to be a jumping off point for further study — not a final word.

"Although the study found that income inequality is associated with later violence, more robust surveillance efforts and further research are needed to understand the psychosocial and physiological mechanisms that explain why children that grow up in more economically unequal settings are at greater risk," the authors conclude.

Something for the journalists in the audience

The association is not between poverty and bullying, it's between inequality and bullying. Elgar offers this for journalists to keep in mind:

"Usually when we think of poverty and inequality, we think about growing up poor. This is the effect of growing up in an unequal setting and it's interesting to think it might change the course of a kid's development."

Citation: J. Elgar, Frank; Gariepy, Genevieve; Dirks, Melanie; Walsh, Sophie D.; Molcho, Michal; Cosma, Alina; Malinowska-Cieslik, Marta; Donnelly, Peter D.; Craig, Wendy. "Association of Early-Life Exposure to Income Inequality With Bullying in Adolescence in 40 Countries," JAMA Pediatrics, May 2019, doi:10.1001/jamapediatrics.2019.1181

13 May 2019

Why do people bully? The scientific reasons

Why do people bully?

According to our latest research, 1 in 2 people have experienced bullying in some form in the last 12-months. And trust us when we say, we know how difficult it can be to go through it, especially if you don't fully understand the psychology of bullying.

In this article, we will be exploring the reasons why people bully, using the latest research and psychology to give you a greater understanding of the motives of those who are either bullying you right now or who have done so in the past.

You may have assumed that you get bullied for whatever makes you different or unique, for example: your race, religion, culture, sexual or gender identity, line of work, fashion sense or weight. By the end of this article, you will know that this is not the case at all.

If you want to talk about it – join our community today to start a conversation about bullying and speak to our amazing digital mentors who can help you anonymously without judgement.

The psychology of being bullied

We will explore the reasons why later on in this article, but most frequently, those who bully others are looking to gain a feeling of power, purpose and control over you.

The easiest way of doing this is to focus on something that is unique about you – either preying on or creating new insecurity with an intent to hurt you either physically or emotionally.

What happens is, we, as the people experiencing bullying, start to internalise it and we become self-critical. We want to understand the reasons why we are being targeted and we start to blame ourselves.

As a result, we try to change or mask that unique characteristic in order to avoid the bullying. We dye our hair, bleach our skin, date people we aren't interested in and cover up our bodies like they are something to be ashamed of.

It starts to affect our behaviour and the ways in which we see ourselves, which in turn, can go on to impact both our mental and physical health.

The way we see bullying is all wrong. It isn't because we are different in some way.

The real reasons why people bully others

In a recent Ditch the Label study, we spoke to 7,347 people about bullying. We asked respondents to define bullying and then later asked if, based on their own definition, they had ever bullied anybody. 14% of our overall sample, so that's 1,239 people, said yes. What we then did was something that had never been done on this scale before; we asked them intimate questions about their lives, exploring things like stress and trauma, home lives, relationships and how they feel about themselves.

In fact, we asked all 7,347 respondents the same questions and then compared the answers from those who had never bullied, those who had bullied at least once and those who bully others daily. This then gave us very strong, scientific and factual data to identify the real reasons why people bully others.

It also scientifically proves that the reason people get bullied is never, contrary to popular belief, because of the unique characteristics of the person experiencing the bullying. So, why do people bully?

Stress and trauma

Our data shows that those who bully are far more likely than average to have experienced a stressful or traumatic situation in the past 5 years. Examples include their parents/guardians splitting up, the death of a relative or the gaining of a little brother or sister.

It makes sense because we all respond to stress in very different ways. Some of us use positive behaviours, such as meditation, exercise and talking therapy – all designed to relieve the stress.

Others use negative behaviours such as bullying, violence and alcohol abuse, which temporarily mask the issues but usually make them worse in the long-term.

The research shows that some people simply do not know how to positively respond to stress and so default to bullying others as a coping mechanism.

Aggressive behaviours

66% of the people who had admitted to bullying somebody else were male. Take a minute to think about how guys are raised in our culture and compare that to the ways in which girls are raised. The moment a guy starts to show any sign of emotion, he's told to man up and to stop being a girl.

For girls, it's encouraged that they speak up about issues that affect them.

For guys, it's discouraged and so they start to respond with aggressive behaviours, such as bullying, as a way of coping with issues that affect them. This is why guys are more likely than girls to physically attack somebody or to commit crimes. It isn't something they are born with, it's a learned behaviour that is actively taught by society using dysfunctional gender norms and roles.

Low self-esteem

In order to mask how they actually feel about themselves, some people who bully focus attention on someone else. They try to avoid any negative attention directed at them by deflecting. But know they might look in the mirror at home and hate the way they look.

There is so much pressure to live up to beauty and fitness standards that we are taught to compare ourselves to others, instead of embracing our own beauty.

They've been bullied

Our research shows that those who have experienced bullying are twice as likely to go on and bully others. Maybe they were bullied as kids in the past, or maybe they are being bullied now.

Often it's used as a defence mechanism and people tend to believe that by bullying others, they will become immune to being bullied themselves. In fact, it just becomes a vicious cycle of negative behaviours.

Difficult home life

1 in 3 of those who bully people daily told us that they feel like their parents/guardians don't have enough time to spend with them. They are more likely to come from larger families and are more likely to live with people other than their biological parents.

There are often feelings of rejection from the very people who should love them unconditionally. They are also much more likely to come from violent households with lots of arguments and hostility.

Low access to education

Without access to education, hate-based conversation directed at others may be the norm. They may not understand what hate speech is and why speaking about people in a derogatory way is not appropriate.

Relationships

Finally, those who bully are more likely to feel like their friendships and family relationships aren't very secure. In order to keep friendships, they might be pressured by their peers to behave in a certain way.

They are more likely to feel like those who are closest to them make them do things that they don't feel comfortable doing and aren't very supportive or loving.

10 September 2020

The above information is reprinted with kind permission from Ditch The Label. ©2021 Ditch The Label Anti-Bullying Charity

www.ditchthelabel.org

Are you a bully without even knowing it? Here's how to tell.

An article from The Conversation.

By Chantal Gautier

THE CONVERSATION

From the playground to parliament, bullying exists everywhere. In fact, a recent report into bullying in the UK's parliament revealed just how serious this problem is, urging behavioural change among MPs. But why is bullying so widespread and difficult to tackle?

Part of the problem is that bullies sometimes don't even realise that they are bullies.

For example, bullying managers may easily justify upsetting certain employees by telling themselves that they are only pushing them to be their best. Or they may be nice to the people they bully at times, and only remember those instances. They may even think that people who break down as a result of their behaviour are not strong enough to work in the profession in question. But how do you know you are actually bullying someone rather than just dealing with an overly sensitive person?

Academics still disagree about how bullying should be conceptualised and defined. The first researcher to investigate bullying – in Norway – used the word "mobbing" to describe it in 1973. Most Western countries have borrowed the English term for bullying, yet this is not always the case.

Bullying may take many forms, from physical assault, verbal abuse and social exclusion to cyber bullying. Generally, to be considered bullying, the practice must be carried out either by an individual or a group, repeatedly over time, and with an intent to hurt an individual person.

The fact that we have no clear definition might explain why it is sometimes difficult to estimate the prevalence of workplace bullying. In 2017, the Workplace Bullying Institute estimated that 60.3m workers in the US alone have been affected by workplace bullying.

In the UK, the Advisory, Conciliation and Arbitration Service (Acas) reported having received 20,000 calls from workers related to bullying and harassment in 2016, many of whom were from an ethnic minority employed in the public sector or women who worked in traditionally male-dominated professions.

The real figures may be distorted as bullying is not always reported, out of fear of retaliation or perhaps because the person affected might not realise they are being bullied.

If your self esteem has been crushed, you may end up blaming yourself, thinking you are worthless and even justify being bullied – not realising you are actually being abused.

Low IQ stereotype

Bullies have traditionally been viewed as having low IQ and being socially inept – lacking in social cognition. We now know that this often isn't the case, but it may contribute to people failing to recognise themselves as bullies.

Some researchers have found evidence that bullies actually score high in their social information processing abilities, as it takes a certain amount of skill to recognise who to target and how. What bullies often do is to seek out people with low self-esteem to pick on. In doing so, they maintain their standing and increase their confidence, which in turn raises their own self-esteem to unrealistically high levels.

However, bullies often lack empathy – a sense of understanding for how those affected might feel when they bully. This could also contribute to them failing to associate their behaviour with bullying. They may intend to hurt an individual in the brief moment they are attacking them, but afterwards tell themselves that it wasn't a big deal, that the victim somehow deserved it or that it was a one off.

Red flags

So how can you know whether you are a bully? It is not possible to "diagnose" in an article such as this, but if you think some of the points below apply to you, it may be worth paying attention to how you are treating others.

- You repeatedly upset someone around you. You may notice this if someone gets angry at you a lot, complains about your behaviour or is tearful often. These reactions are indeed a red flag and should be taken seriously.

- You have a lack of empathy. This is not always easy to recognise in oneself. You may want to ask people around you whether they think that is the case, or even take an empathy test.

- You can get aggressive. This may include openly shouting, threatening or humiliating someone in front of others. But it could also be passive aggressive comments, such as "Oh, you are doing it that way, that's brave."

- You thrive around insecure people. If you make yourself feel better by evoking discomfort or insecurity in a colleague, that would be a classic sign of bullying. This could be done, for example, by persistently picking on someone or deliberately setting them up to fail.

- You spread malicious rumours about a staff member. It may not seem like a big deal, but spreading rumours could make someone's life a living hell – costing them professional and social success.

- You misuse your power or position about performance issues. For example, you may intentionally block someone's promotion or take away duties and responsibilities without any rationale or substance. Other possibilities include deliberately and persistently ignoring or excluding someone from joint collaborations and social events.

Bullying is especially likely to take place in stressful workplaces with poor leadership and a culture that rewards aggressive, competitive behaviour. We know that bullying can trigger an array of mental health issues including depression, burnout, increased absenteeism, low self-confidence and stress.

Employers who do not provide a safe environment for their employees are in fact breaking the law. While most countries have some sort of policy on tackling bullying in place (including Canada, Australia, the Netherlands, Sweden, France and Denmark) we need a greater global push to recognise how widespread the problem is.

Educating people about bullying is a positive step forward. This will also create a safer environment for victims to come forward. Hopefully, the change brought about by the #metoo movement with regards to sexual harassment will soon spread to include bullying. In the meantime, we should all make sure we are doing everything we can to treat others with respect.

1 November 2018

Instagram to warn users over 'bullying' language in captions

'We should all consider the impact of our words,' says anti-cyberbullying charity.

By Sabrina Barr

Instagram is to warn its users when they are using language in their captions that may be perceived as offensive or bullying.

The social media company said it will use artificial intelligence to spot language in captions that could be deemed potentially harmful.

A similar feature, which alerts users when the comments they're leaving on other people's posts contain possibly harmful language, was launched earlier this year.

When an Instagram user posts a caption that could be seen as bullying, a message will appear on their screen informing them that their caption looks similar to others that have previously been reported on the platform.

They are then given the option to edit the caption, learn more about why it has been flagged by the feature or to post it as it is.

Earlier this year, the head of Instagram Adam Mosseri published a statement outlining the Facebook-owned firm's commitment to combatting cyberbullying.

"We can do more to prevent bullying from happening on Instagram, and we can do more to empower the targets of bullying to stand up for themselves," he said.

"It's our responsibility to create a safe environment on Instagram. This has been an important priority for us for some time, and we are continuing to invest in better understanding and tackling this problem."

Instagram has been criticised in the past for failing to take adequate measures to protect its users from online abuse.

In February, the social media company stated it was committed to removing all images related to self-harm on the platform.

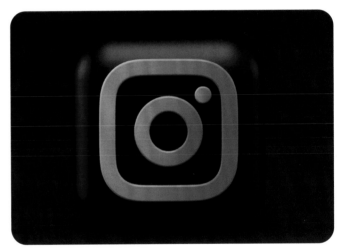

Eight months later, Instagram announced plans to extend its ban on selfharm- and suicide-related images to drawings, cartoons and memes.

Dan Raisbeck, co-founder of anti-cyberbullying charity Cybersmile, said the firm's latest feature is a good example of taking a proactive approach to preventing cyberbullying.

"We should all consider the impact of our words, especially online where comments can be easily misinterpreted," he said.

"Tools like Instagram's Comment and Caption Warning are a useful way to encourage that behaviour before something is posted, rather than relying on reactive action to remove a hurtful comment after it's been seen by others."

16 November 2019

Mental health and bullying

One in four people experience a mental health problem. Whilst not all are down to bullying behaviour, simply having a mental health problem can lead to a person being bullied.

As we come to better understand bullying, the more concerned health professionals are becoming over the potentially damaging and long-lasting impact that bullying has on the mental health of those who experience it.

Bullying can devastate a person's life. They can lose all faith in their ability, feel ill and depressed and find it hard to feel motivated to work or learn.

Those who are bullied are at risk for a variety of mental health concerns. Some of them are at risk for experiencing an acute stress or trauma reaction, or depending on the form of bullying, they could have Post Traumatic Stress Disorder (PTSD). Young people who are bullied are more likely to experience: depression, anxiety, increased feelings of sadness and loneliness, changes in sleep and eating patterns and loss of interest in activities they used to enjoy. Bullying also causes long-term damage to a person's self-esteem.

There is some research that indicates that some young people who are bullies, are at increased risk for substance use, academic problems and violence to others later in life. The research also indicates that those who are bullied who then go on to bully, are at greater risk for mental health problems.

Bullying which is not responded to effectively, can cause children and young people to develop other coping strategies such as self-isolation or self-harm and cause significant disruption to their ability to engage with school, learning and their wider relationships. Anxiety problems are thought to affect up to 1 in 6 young people and include social phobias, generalised anxiety problems, panic attacks and obsessive compulsive disorder.

Mental health problems are not always apparent and can often be overlooked in schools. In addition, problems can be complex, with many of those experiencing mental health problems having difficulties in more than one area (e.g. conduct problems and depression). As such, professionals working with young people who have obvious behavioural difficulties should also consider whether they are masking additional emotional problems.

Young people are much more likely to have symptoms of depression and anxiety if they have either been bullied or engaged in bullying others when compared to young people who have not been involved in bullying. It is well recognised in research that young people who have been bullied are more likely to have lower self-esteem and self-confidence. In particular, sustained, prolonged bullying focusing on a particular aspect of someone's identity, which

The cycle of bullying and mental health issues

There is a strong link between bullying and mental health. This diagram shows those who suffer from bullying are more ilkely to expereince mental health issues and those who have mental issues are more likely to be bullied.

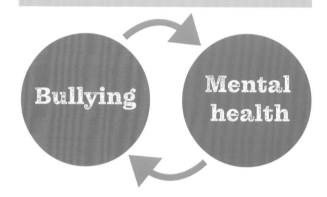

People are more likely to develop mental health issues if they are bullied

Bullying ⟷ Mental health

People with mental health issues are more likely to be bullied

goes unrecognised or unchallenged, may have significant effects on the mental health of young people and may lead them to develop a negative self-identity.

If a person is being bullied at work, it can be difficult for them to know what to do.

Sometimes bullying may be obvious, but sometimes it can be very covert and harder to identify. Being bullied at work can make a person's life miserable. They can lose all faith in their ability, feel ill, anxious, stressed and be unable to motivate themselves to go to work. With 1 in 3 adults bullied at work and stress being the biggest reason for sickness absenteeism in the workplace, we must never underestimate the damage bullying does to a person's mental health.

We need to be more aware of the damage bullying causes. We need to speak out more when we see it happening. We need to do this because it saves lives.

Cyber-bullying is children's greatest online fear, according to NSPCC

More than a quarter of children across the UK said bullying or someone being unkind to them was what worried them most online.

By Will Hazell

Being cyber-bullied is children's greatest fear when they go online, according to a survey conducted on behalf of the NSPCC and O2.

More than a quarter of children (27 per cent) across the UK said bullying or someone being unkind to them was what worried them the most when using the internet.

The survey by Chrysalis Research of more than 4,000 children aged eight to 13 found being contacted by someone they don't know was the second biggest online concern (16 per cent of respondents).

The poll was carried out ahead of Tuesday's Safer Internet Day.

'So humiliated'

One teenage girl confided to a Childline counsellor about her experience of cybe-rbullying.

"I met them online on this game and we were friends at first but then it all turned nasty," she said.

"He says some really bad stuff to me and makes me feel so rubbish about myself. I feel so humiliated because other people on the site see it and then join in. I don't know what to do."

Childline provided 15,851 counselling sessions last year in relation to online and face-to-face bullying.

'Sadfishing'

Cyber-bullying also seems to be a constantly changing phenomenon. A report by Digital Awareness UK in October highlighted how some vulnerable young people who go online to seek support can find themselves being bullied and accused of "sadfishing" – a mocking accusation that they are exaggerating their problems in order to gain attention.

The NSPCC and O2 survey found that speaking to parents or carers is overwhelmingly seen by children (89 per cent) as the thing to do to help them stay safe online.

But an additional survey of about 4,700 parents and carers found that only 35 per cent said their children had raised internet safety with them in the past 12 months.

And the survey found that while 92 per cent of parents felt they knew how to advise their child on staying safe online, less than half (42 per cent) had agreed guidelines on what they do when using the internet.

Regular conversations

Laura Randall, associate head of child safety online and innovation at the NSPCC, said:

"Children and young people are becoming increasingly aware of the risks they face when going online and the vital role their parents or carers can play in ensuring they stay safe."

She added: "As a result, parents and carers need to take the initiative and set up regular conversations with their child about their online life."

The NSPCC and O2 have published an "online family agreement" for parents and children to fill in and sign together to help encourage more regular conversations about internet safety.

It contains suggestions for promises that children and parents should make to one other – for example that a child will check with their parents before they download a new app.

10 February 2020

Social media use in teens linked to cyberbullying and less sleep and exercise

Facebook and Instagram are damaging children's mental health," reports the Sun as a new study suggests there's a link between frequent social media use and poor mental health and wellbeing in teens.

Researchers analysed data from 12,866 young people aged 13 to 16 in England.

The researchers used the information, collected in 3 waves from 2013 to 2015, to assess the link between social media use and health.

But the social media channels themselves may not be to blame.

Researchers found that, particularly among girls, much of the association between frequent use of social media and poor mental health or wellbeing could be explained by cyberbullying, lack of sleep and reduced physical activity.

They suggested that limiting access to social media might not be the best way to improve teenagers' wellbeing.

Instead, it might be more effective to decrease cyberbullying or increase resilience to it, and make sure teenagers get enough sleep and physical activity.

Where did the story come from?

The researchers who carried out the study were from the University College London, Great Ormond Street Institute of Child Health and Hammersmith Hospital.

No funding was reported for the research.

It was published in the peer-reviewed journal The Lancet: Child & Adolescent Health. While most of the reports in the UK media include the information about cyberbullying and lack of sleep, several sources suggest that use of social media makes these things inevitable.

For example, the Sun said: "Social media use exposes teenagers to cyberbullying, harms sleep and stops them exercising."

Many of the headlines on the stories tend to overstate the risks associated with social media, while most of the articles gave more nuanced explanations of the study results.

What kind of research was this?

This was a secondary analysis of a cohort study.

Cohort studies are good ways to spot patterns between factors, such as social media use, sleep, cyberbullying and mental health.

But they do not explain the relationship between factors, such as whether one directly causes another.

Secondary analysis means that this is a new analysis of research that's already been published, rather than a study set up specifically to answer these questions.

What did the research involve?

Researchers used information from the Our Futures study, which questioned 12,866 children from 866 secondary schools across the UK in 3 waves:

- in 2013, when they were aged 13 to 14
- in 2014, when they were aged 14 to 15
- in 2015, when they were aged 15 to 16

In 2013, teenagers were asked about their social media use, but not about their mental health or wellbeing.

In 2014, they were asked to fill in a questionnaire that assessed mental health and psychological distress (GHQ12).

In 2015, they filled in Office for National Statistics questionnaires about their life satisfaction, wellbeing, happiness and anxiety.

Social media use was categorised by frequency of use, with "very frequent" use meaning that they checked into social media sites 3 times a day or more.

Researchers looked at the link between social media frequency of use from 2013 onwards and how it was related to mental health in 2014 and wellbeing in 2015.

They then looked at known factors that can also affect mental health and wellbeing, and that have been linked previously to social media use.

These factors were cyberbullying, sleep duration and physical activity.

Children were asked about these in 2014, and also asked about cyberbullying in 2013.

The researchers adjusted the figures on social media use to see how much of the effect on mental health and wellbeing could be explained by these other factors.

They did the analyses separately for girls and boys.

What were the basic results?

As they expected, researchers found "very frequent" social media use was linked to poorer mental health and wellbeing.

"Very frequent" use rose from 42.6% in 2013 to 68.5% in 2015, and was more common among girls.

In 2014, 19.0% of children were psychologically distressed, according to their GHQ12 score:

♦ 27.5% of girls who used social media very frequently had a score indicating psychological distress. Compared with those who used social media once daily, frequent users were more likely to have psychological distress after taking into account other factors (adjusted odds ratio (aOR) 1.31, 95% confidence interval (CI) 1.06 to 1.63)

♦ 14.9% of boys who used social media very frequently had a score indicating psychological distress. Again, compared with those who used social media once daily, frequent users were more likely to have psychological distress after taking into account other factors (aOR 1.67, 95% CI 1.24 to 2.26)

But once cyberbullying, sleep duration and physical activity were taken into account, the link between social media use and psychological distress for girls and boys was much weaker.

Cyberbullying seemed to have the biggest effect on psychological distress, followed by lack of sleep.

Similar results were found for wellbeing for girls, who showed decreased life satisfaction and happiness, and increased anxiety, if they were very frequent users of social media.

But there was no link between wellbeing and social media frequency of use for boys.

When cyberbullying, sleep and physical activity were taken into account, the link between social media use and wellbeing for girls disappeared completely, with cyberbullying and sleep again the most important factors.

How did the researchers interpret the results?

The researchers said: "Although very frequent social media use predicted later poor mental health and wellbeing in both sexes … this association among girls appeared to be largely mediated through cyberbullying and inadequate sleep, with inadequate physical activity playing a more minor role."

They added: "Our data suggest that interventions to reduce social media use to improve mental health might be misplaced.

"Preventative efforts should consider interventions to prevent or increase resilience to cyberbullying and to ensure adequate sleep and physical activity in young people."

Conclusion

New technologies always bring anxiety about their potential dangers. But it may not be the technologies themselves that are harmful, so much as the way we use them.

Bullying in childhood is hardly new, but social media is a new platform for bullying.

It makes sense that using social media frequently might expose a child to bullying, which has a negative impact on mental health.

Lack of sleep can also damage mental health, especially over the long term, and children and teenagers need more sleep than adults.

If children are awake late into the night using social media, that's likely to cause problems, as it would if they were awake late doing other things.

This study had limitations, but it does help us to understand how technologies may be affecting children, rather than assuming it's something intrinsic to the technology that's causing the harm.

The study did not measure children's mental health or wellbeing at the start, so we do not know whether their mental wellbeing increased or decreased over time.

It could be that children who were already unhappy used social media more than their happier peers.

The study also relied on children self-reporting their social media use by how many times a day they looked at sites.

Many people look at sites far more often than 3 times a day, so the measure for "very frequent use" is not particularly precise.

And we do not know what sort of cyberbullying was taking place, or how often children experienced it.

Although the study does not suggest limiting social media use overall, it would make sense to try to limit the use of social media overnight (for example, by discouraging teens from taking phones into the bedroom) to help teenagers get enough sleep.

Supporting children who may be subjected to cyberbullying would also be a useful step, starting by finding out whether a child is being affected by this type of bullying.

14 August 2019

We don't know the true extent of cyberbullying – and children need help dealing with it.

An article from The Conversation.

By Peter Macauley

THE CONVERSATION

There are growing fears about the rise of cyberbullying and its impact on children. Unlike traditional face-to-face bullying, a bully can conceal their identity online and target their victims constantly without the limits of location or time.

A lack of reporting of cyberbullying and its low visibility when compared to face-to-face bullying make it difficult to gauge its true extent and impact. However, investigating rates of cyberbullying is extremely complex.

Teachers regard cyberbullying to be more serious than face-to-face bullying because there are always new ways for children to bully online through new apps and technologies, making it difficult to identify and respond to cyberbullying. Young people also believe that cyberbullying is more serious and more problematic in the school environment than face-to-face bullying.

However, it is difficult to truly assess how widespread cyberbullying is. It has been shown that children report cyberbullying less due to fear of consequences. Children's

worries include that telling someone about cyberbullying will make the situation worse or lead to the confiscation of their electronic devices. They are also concerned about not knowing what the repercussions of reporting cyberbullying might be.

This research may qualify the findings of a recent Ofcom report, which suggests that cyberbullying is not more of a widespread problem than real-life bullying. The report found that older children aged 12-15 are just as likely to experience "real life" bullying as bullying on social media. Younger children aged eight to 11 were found to be more likely to experience traditional bullying (14%) than online bullying (8%).

Previous research has also found that traditional bullying takes place more often than cyberbullying. A 2017 study in England of 120,115 15-year-olds found rates of traditional bullying to be far higher. Less than 1% of the teenagers said they had experienced cyberbullying only, while 27% had faced traditional bullying – and 3% said they had encountered both types.

These findings run counter to the perceptions of teachers and children. Bullying is also more visible in the physical world and more likely to be noticed by teachers in the school environment. Teachers are less likely to notice and identify cyberbullying.

The bystander effect

The role of bystanders who get involved has been shown to be crucial in stopping bullying. Here, too, there are differences between online and offline cases. Children report that bystanders are more likely to get involved to stop traditional bullying than for cyberbullying incidents. They considered the reason to be the physical presence of authority figures in the real world.

Social psychological research suggests the presence of other onlookers tends to reduce a person's willingness to intervene in a positive way: "there's no need for me to help since someone else will." This is known as the "diffusion of responsibility". This theory suggests that people are less likely to intervene in online bullying because of the potential greater number of virtual onlookers. The case of Canadian 14-year-old Carson Crimeni, whose death was broadcast on the internet, is a tragic example.

On the other hand, the online environment provides increased anonymity and autonomy to young people. My research suggests that children themselves are more likely to intervene in cyberbullying than traditional bullying. This research also found that children intervene in online bullying more when the incident is severe, suggesting that "diffusion of responsibility" may also be influenced by how serious the incident is perceived to be.

Tackling cyberbullying

Despite widespread concern about cyberbullying, children lack knowledge of how to stay safe online – for instance by not giving out personal information or by using blocking and reporting tools. For example, in my recent study conducted in the UK, children were found to be complacent about this issue. Children think they know how to stay safe online, but struggled to actually articulate ways to do this. This might leave some children vulnerable and make risks more likely to lead to harm.

Teachers may also lack the skills to deal with cyberbullying. My research has found that many recognise it to be a problem and feel they have a responsibility to address it and educate young people about appropriate online behaviour, but fewer felt confident about how to address the issue.

The NSPCC, Anti-Bullying Alliance, and Diana Award have teamed up to launch a national campaign called Stop, Speak, Support to encourage children to think critically about what they see online and speak out when necessary.

The Ofcom report found that approximately a fifth of children aged eight to 15 are bullied in some way. In order to counter the effects of bullying we need to promote intervention. Those who witness bullying as well as figures of authority such as teachers should be encouraged to take responsibility for addressing it both in "real life" and in the online world.

24 February 2020

'It's had a lasting impact': students on being bullied over their accents

Past and present university students talk about their experiences of being made to feel out of place.

By Nazia Parveen North of England correspondent

A Guardian investigation has found widespread evidence of students being ridiculed over their accents and backgrounds at some of the country's leading universities. Here, students past and present reflect on their experiences:

'It made me feel like I did not belong'

Nina White, 26, from Stockton-on-Tees, studied English and theatre at the University of Warwick

"It sounds ridiculous, but I only realised I had what people regarded as a strong regional accent when I first began my undergraduate studies. Mocking of my accent was immediate and I was shocked at the perceptions of people from the north-east. The perception of me was that if I had a drink I would become aggressive and scrappy, and this was all because I was from the north. I am neither of those things.

"One flatmate once asked me in genuine amazement: 'You have BBC up where you're from?' I had to laugh, but looking back this moment neatly encapsulated the social position that many people imagined northern towns to be in. These little experiences made me feel like I did not belong at my university, that I'd gotten there by mistake. A feeling of otherness, imposter syndrome.

"Fellow students expressed incredulity that I had made it top of the class in my first year. This incredulity rubbed off on me. Even when I graduated with first-class honours I was certain that I would never want to return to a university again.

"Two years later, after living in another northern city, I had recovered my confidence and started my master's at the University of Liverpool. Here, I felt none of that regional prejudice, neither at work nor in my studies.

"At Teesside University, where I am completing a PhD, there is a huge proportion of local students and staff too, which is so refreshing and reassuring. Here I am no different. I am at home."

'The way students talked about me was truly intolerable'

Christopher Burden, 24, from the Black Country, studied modern languages at the University of Birmingham

"My experience of university was a constant barrage of abuse from students and staff who were verbally disapproving of my mild but noticeable Black Country accent. This manifested itself in various ways. Staff on more than one occasion said 'we don't normally get your type here' or 'perhaps you could try and fit in'. The staff were completely misguided, but with students it was different.

"Broadly, my course was made up of people who failed to get into Oxford or Cambridge, so there was an elitist atmosphere as many of them had been to school at places like Eton and Harrow. I went to a regular comprehensive in Wolverhampton and this seemed really unusual to them.

"After peer-assessed presentations I became very used to negative feedback where they would say they couldn't understand me. Students would also regularly announce that they didn't want to work with me because I would somehow bring down their grade because of my background.

"It feels weird to talk about bullying as an adult, but ultimately the way students talked about me, dreaded having me in a presentation group and otherwise judged me for being working class was truly intolerable at times.

"The whole demoralising episode has had a lasting impact. It knocked my confidence and I began trying to hide my accent. I have always been proud of where I am from but the kind of people that mocked me at university are the kind of people that will be recruiters for jobs . It has inhibited me, definitely.

"I am gay and if anyone makes homophobic remarks towards me it is considered illegal, but if someone is classist I can't say anything because it is not a protected characteristic – yet it is still abuse."

'I can still hear her clipped RP echoing in my ears'

Rachael Drew, 35, from Scarborough, studied drama and theatre arts at Queen Margaret University in Edinburgh

"'You'll never get anywhere talking like that, it makes you sound stupid. You need to try and flatten your Yorkshire accent.' That was a member of staff in my third year of university. I tried to not to cry, and sort of managed, crumbling completely when I left the room. What could I say to that? They must be right. They knew what they were talking about.

"My experience at university had generally been fantastic. Obviously I got a ribbing from my peers about words like purple, bus or murder, but you sort of expect that anywhere outside of the region. Pals were playful. Maybe that's why that one session with that tutor always stands out in my mind. I can still hear her clipped received pronunciation echoing in my ears.

"'When you use "like" in sentences, you sound like a teenager. No one will take you seriously.' I didn't argue. I should have argued. Instead I gave them too much sway and tried to follow their instruction. My accent completely changed during my four years at university, flattening back immediately when I was welcomed home. It's really hard to speak when your voice will put you at the back of the intellectual queue. Now, 13 years later, although I do catch myself saying 'like' all the time, I try to let that anger charge me rather than choke me."

'I remember feeling overwhelmingly exposed'

Emily Northorpe, 23, from South Tyneside, studied English literature at Durham University

"It's a strange experience to be in a northern city with a northern accent but to be in the minority or to feel embarrassed about it. I remember remarks people made about being sick of hearing northern accents when they were out and about in town. The feeling of ridicule or judgment would be particularly noticeable in academic settings like seminars or tutorials.

"I purposefully did not speak out of fear, despite having done all the preparatory reading. It can be such a debilitating feeling when you want to join in the debate and offer analysis but you daren't because you're worried, not about what you're saying, but how you're saying it. My anxiety would ripple through my body if a tutor called on me for my opinion. There would be a look or a smirk from the other students and I just remember feeling overwhelmingly exposed.

"It tainted my whole experience of being at university and made me completely go into my shell. I would become mute in social situations and academic settings. To be the odd one out in a place that was very close, geographically, to my family home was so strange."

'What will it be like in the workplace?'

Olivia Allen, 18, from Birmingham, is studying politics, sociology and Russian at the University of Exeter

"Since moving down south a month ago I can think of at least 10 occasions when my accent, being a relatively strong one from Birmingham, has been brought up and mocked in conversation. Most notably, my peers in politics modules specifically have said they'd never have guessed I'd want to take a subject like politics, and that I should speak more eloquently if I want to be taken seriously.

"I got three A*'s and one A in my A-levels, and nothing below an A equivalent in my GCSEs. I shouldn't have to speak more eloquently to be listened to when I know the worth of what I'm saying regardless of my accent.

"I've lived in Birmingham my whole life and I'm not ashamed of the accent I have. I've had people make assumptions about my intelligence, family background and financial situation based on nothing but the way I speak, and while I know they're unfounded, I still can't believe this is something I'm dealing with at all.

"I have always been quite self-confident but this has made me think. If this is what is happening at university, what will it be like going forward, in the workplace? Will I be judged on factors that I can't control?"

24 October 2020

Bullying is driving more than one in eight young people to have suicidal behaviours, research shows

Scientists looked at data from 220,000 adolescents from 83 countries around the world.

By Shaun Lintern, Health Correspondent

Bullying is a key driver of suicidal behaviour among young people across the world, according to new research warning the problem is worse than previously feared.

An international study by scientists in Britain, China and the US looked at data from 220,000 adolescents aged between 12 and 15 from 83 countries.

The study found more than one in eight youngsters across the world had suicidal behaviours, with bullying strongly associated to suicide attempts.

The study, led by scientists at the University of Wolverhampton, and China's Guangzhou Medical University, said there was a need to strengthen policies and actions to reduce bullying in order to address suicidal behaviours among young people.

Worldwide each year, approximately 800,000 people die by suicide, the second leading cause of death among 10 to 24-year-olds. Child suicide is linked to 220,000 deaths a year.

The research, published in The Lancet journal EClinicalMedicine, said the association between bullying and behaviours such as suicidal planning and attempts varied by region.

The strongest link between bullying and contemplating suicide was found in Southeast Asia, and for suicidal planning and attempts in western Pacific countries.

Bullied boys were more likely to attempt suicide than bullied girls.

Across the 83 countries, the highest risks for suicidal behaviours was in African nations. Overall, more than a third of adolescents were being bullied.

Dr James Tang, an author of the paper, said: "Compared with findings of previous studies, our study demonstrated higher levels of suicidal ideation, planning and attempts in adolescents worldwide, particularly suicidal attempts.

"Also, the association of being bullied with suicide attempts is the strongest one, suggesting that any laws, policies and interventions used to reduce or stop bullying among adolescents could have greater effects on suicide reduction. Suicidal attempts in adolescents needs to be prioritised for prevention and treatment since its ratio to completed suicides is high at about 20:1."

Professor Ruoling Chen, professor of public health and medical statistics from the University of Wolverhampton, added: "The prevalence of suicidal behaviours and being bullied in adolescents varied across countries and World Health Organization regions significantly.

"In the Africa region the increased risk of suicidal behaviours among adolescents could be explained by poverty, political unrest, infectious diseases, while the high level of being bullied could be partly ascribed to low socio-economic status of adolescents, poor school, home and social environment, political violence, war and crime.

"The findings of this study could provide the basis for the development of regional or national suicide prevention strategies in adolescents."

For confidential support call Samaritans on 116 123.

11 January 2020

Workplace bullying like persistent fault-finding and demeaning behaviour destroys lives – here's how to fight back

Devaluing and demeaning behaviour by a colleague are all ways in which the office, factory or even Parliament can turn into a nightmare.

By Etan Smallman

In an era of corporate social responsibility, workplace wellness initiatives and even "chief happiness officers", one age-old problem stubbornly refuses to pivot, evolve and, going forward, undergo a much-needed paradigm shift: workplace bullying.

Workplace bullying can seriously harm workers' mental and physical health. Not to mention their productivity and a company's bottom line.

Yet a quarter of employees think their organisation turns a blind eye to the issue, according to a report in January by the Chartered Institute of Personnel and Development. It found that half of victims did not report their bullying or harassment.

It also found that the groups most likely to become victims are black and Asian employees, women, and those with a disability. The Trades Union Congress (TUC) found that one in four workers has been bullied in the past five years.

Workplace bullying at the heart of government

It's a problem that even extends to the heart of government. Last week, Home Secretary Priti Patel was accused of bullying behaviour towards staff. Former ministers and civil servants also alleged "aggressive" and "vile" conduct when she was in charge of the Department for International Development. Patel vehemently denies this.

In January, former House of Commons Speaker John Bercow was the subject of a formal complaint by former Clerk of the House Lord Lisvane. Lord Lisvane alleged he had bullied staff. Mr Bercow "categorically" denies the allegations. And Dawn Butler, a candidate for the deputy Labour leadership, suggested the denial of a peerage for the former Speaker is "a form of bullying too".

Also last month, Kirsty Buchanan, a senior civil servant at the Ministry of Housing, Communities and Local Government, was suspended amid allegations of bullying.

A toxic bullying culture

Meanwhile, the Movement for Reform Judaism pledged to establish a "robust and transparent" code of conduct for its religious leaders. It came in the wake of a storm about allegations of bullying and inappropriate behaviour against a rabbi who was subsequently promoted. He denies the allegations.

And the first annual report by Her Majesty's Inspectorate of Constabulary and Fire and Rescue Services found "a toxic, bullying culture". In one service, 46 per cent of employees said they felt bullied or harassed at work. "Disturbingly, some people we spoke to seemed to find the poor treatment of staff by other colleagues amusing," the report said.

A TUC survey of its safety representatives last year found that they regarded bullying as the second biggest workplace issue after stress. They reported it to be worst in local and central government (cited by, respectively, 80 per cent and 71 per cent of respondents).

Workplace bullying even inspired an ITV drama in December. Mike Bartlett is the writer of Sticks and Stones. He said: "We certainly could all be good bullies, and actually probably the majority of people have been."

Defining workplace bullying

Sir Cary Cooper is professor of organisational psychology at Manchester Business School, and author of Wellbeing at Work. He has been studying workplace bullying for decades. He defines the behaviour as "persistent demeaning and devaluing of an individual in the workplace". Usually, he says, as the result of what he calls a "command-and-control" culture.

Managing somebody "by fault-finding rather than by providing them with constructive feedback" is a typical manifestation. "Normally the single biggest category of bullying is a boss to a subordinate," he says. "But it can be between colleagues. It can be the subordinate – who doesn't want to be managed – to their boss. It can be from a client."

Indeed, the TUC reports that nine per cent of senior managers surveyed said they had been targeted by bullies in the previous nine months.

Sir Cary has found that victims of workplace bullying have significantly more sickness absence days than others. But the impact goes even wider. "We found something interesting that we didn't anticipate," he says. The mental health of staff

members who witness another person being bullied at work is also affected, and they also take more sick leave.

"So we have another category, called passive or secondary bullying. You aren't being bullied but those around you are and it's making you feel insecure because you may feel you're next."

How bullies become bosses

It is a problem that was highlighted last month by a survey of 4,200 people working in British science labs. It found that 43 per cent had been personally bullied, while 61 per cent had witnessed workplace bullying.

But just 37 per cent would feel comfortable reporting a case, according to a report by Wellcome, Britain's largest charity. The report spoke of "a culture where bullying was tolerated as long as funding and outputs remained high".

Sir Cary believes the main failure of organisations is people being promoted to managerial jobs "based on their technical skills, not their people skills".

"Say you're a great engineer and the only way you're going to earn more money in the firm is by applying for a management job – but you're really poor with people. I think the bulk of the bullies are people who get into a role, particularly in managing other human beings, and they're not competent, interested or skilled to do so."

The end of a dream job

Peter* was delighted to win his dream job in broadcasting in 2017. But after starting a new shift pattern, he began to feel personally targeted by his new boss.

"She would shout at me if I made mistakes," he tells i. "When I answered the phone, she'd be in my other ear putting me off.

"I brought it up with my manager quite early on and they felt that I needed training. There was no mention that she might be in the wrong or an apology for what I had gone through. This went on for a good few months and eventually I was taken off the shift completely.

"I was advised by Citizens Advice to join and speak to the union representatives. But the most bizarre thing was, the person who was bullying me was the union rep. I've since left that job and turned my back on the whole business. I made sure that I sent an email to all the managers and HR. It's a real shame that it ended the way it did, because it had been my dream to work for this company for a long time."

Peter says his advice to others in a similar situation would be: "Do not let it kill your spirit. People who do this are usually very insecure about something or just jealous that they aren't you. It's not nice, but just focus on your task and make sure you are being flawless."

What companies can do

Sir Cary believes companies must not merely have a safe reporting system for workplace bullying and then wait for complaints before taking action. He says that "wellbeing audits" can pinpoint an area of concern before anyone raises the alarm.

"Look at what's causing people to get ill at work, and look at employees' perception of their roles, managers and colleagues. And if you aggregate the data in an organisation, you can say: that bit over there has a bullying management style and culture, and we have to deal with it."

Technological solutions may also offer some hope. Spot is an artificial intelligence "chatbot" that allows employees to accurately and securely document harassment. It produces a time-stamped interview that they can save just for themselves or submit to their human resources department.

Users can follow up on reports – even if they were submitted anonymously. The software, according to its co-creator, helps "turn a memory into evidence".

Another system, Botler AI, asks for an anonymous incident report. It analyses this before emailing back with related sections of the law and legal precedents that may be relevant.

It also offers supportive, judgment-free responses, such as: "Sexual harassment is inexcusable, and I'm really sorry if you've had to deal with it. My aim is to empower you by teaching you what your rights are."

Workplace bullying — your rights

Harassment at work is unlawful under the Equality Act 2010. It can include spreading malicious rumours, unfair treatment or unfairly denying someone's training or promotion opportunities. Acas (The Advisory, Conciliation and Arbitration Service) says bullying can also include someone regularly putting you down in meetings or your team never letting you join social events.

Government advice is to see if you can sort it out informally first. Then report the bullying to your manager, human resources department or trade union representative. If this does not work, you can make a formal complaint. Use your employer's grievance procedure. If this fails, you can take legal action at an employment tribunal.

If trying to resolve the problem with the bully face to face, Acas advises you to explain how their behaviour makes you feel. Be firm, not aggressive. And stick to the facts.

Your employer has a legal duty to protect you. "If you have to leave your job because of severe bullying that your employer did nothing about, you might be able to claim constructive dismissal," says Acas.

Life after workplace bullying

Such smart solutions may be grounds for optimism for the likes of Colette McKune. She was the victim of bullying at a former company about 20 years ago. But she says she has since noticed a discernible shift in workplace culture.

"I reported discrimination. It turned out to be a mistake. The discrimination quickly progressed to outright bullying. I tried to resist leaving. But after 18 months of it, I had become so disillusioned that I left the sector I worked within," Ms McKune says.

She is now group chief executive of national social purpose organisation ForViva. "Of course, people should report it today. Thankfully, the business environment has changed since then."

* Name changed to protect identity

25 February 2020

Over 70% of UK employees have been bullied at work in the last three years finds new study

By Calvin Barnett

A new study has revealed the extent of bullying in the workplace with over a third of employees in the UK revealing that they have experienced or witnessed bullying at work over the past three years.

The research, conducted by Employment law specialists Kew Law, asked employees of 131 companies in the UK whether they had been bullied or witnessed bullying in the workplace, and 71 per cent said yes.

35 per cent of respondents said that they had been direct victims of workplace bullying themselves.

According to the findings, the most commonly identified form of bullying in the workplace by 27 per cent of those who participated in the study was overloading individuals with work.

20 per cent highlighted that they had been witness to or victim of unfair treatment whilst 18 per cent emphasised picking on or regularly undermining someone.

16 per cent noted the spread of malicious rumours as a common form of bullying, and the same percentage also identified ignoring and excluding someone's contribution as well.

In addition, 7 per cent of respondents picked up on the denial of someone's training or promotion opportunities as a commonplace bullying tactic as well.

According to Kew Law, These align closely with the government's definitions of bullying in the workplace.

When broken down into demographics, the figures show a general decrease in the likelihood of bullying as age increases – with only 23 per cent of 45-54 year olds saying they have experienced bullying, compared with 44 per cent of 21-24 year olds.

In addition, 40 per cent of female respondents said they had been bullied, compared with 31 per cent of male respondents. 67 per cent of employees at director level had been bullied, making them the most likely category to be targeted.

Of those who had been bullied, 60% were bullied to the extent that their productivity was affected, they took time off work, or they even left the company. 13% resigned altogether, while 28% took leave, and 15% took unpaid leave, as a result of the bullying. This shows not only that bullying seriously impacts an individual's ability to do their job, and in turn affects the productivity of the wider business, but that companies are not doing enough to keep bullied employees in the office, in either the short or long term.

Karen Kwong, Director of Renoc Consulting and an Organisational Psychologist and wellbeing coach, commented on the findings: "Bullying can be extremely damaging for an employee. On an individual level, they are likely to lose motivation and confidence in themselves, suffer from severe anxiety and stress which in turn could lead to more serious mental and physical illnesses. This, in turn, might lead to their work suffering too, through no fault of their own.

"The individual may also start losing faith in the team, the manager and the organisation which is bad for overall morale and the reputation of any firm. These days things like Glassdoor and social media can very quickly ruin reputations of even the most reputable of businesses."

Alongside identifying regular forms of bullying experienced in companies, the study also highlighted the need for some HR departments to improve how they handle cases of workplace bullying.

22 per cent of respondents said the bullying was not dealt with despite raising it with HR, and only 11 per cent of respondents felt that the situation then improved after doing so.

35 per cent of respondents who had been bullied in the workplace said that a greater amount of confidentiality should have been upheld throughout the handling of the issue whilst 26 per cent felt that better communication was needed from the company on what constitutes unacceptable behaviour in the workplace.

In addition, despite 13 per cent having left a job because of bullying, just 4 per cent raised the issue with HR before doing so.

Given the very real impact of workplace bullying on long-term mental health, these figures suggest that not only do HR departments need to overhaul their grievance procedures, but make themselves much more approachable too, suggests Kew Law.

"Procedures are vital, as are ways in which to escalate and report such complaints objectively. Often, people who have been bullied don't want to say anything because they fear reprisals – a very real issue," continued Karen.

"HR is often powerless to do much if the bully is a powerful decision-maker or moneymaker in the organisation. This is why to me, it should start from the top, the culture should be one of respect cascading all the way down to all levels. Then it is less likely to happen. And if it does, it will be swiftly and effectively handled in a fair and objective manner."

The survey also attempted to find out how companies can improve their response to bullying.

Up to 46 per cent of employees surveyed said they would not report bullying behaviour with either the HR department or senior management, and 33 per cent would rather take it up with the bully directly than raise it with HR.

The research reinforces that bullying is not taken seriously enough in the eyes of employees, stated Kew Law, and that HR teams should better encourage the reporting of bullying behaviour when it is observed.

27 April 2020

Spotting the signs of Gaslighting

Subtle workplace bullying also known as Gaslighting.

By Christine Pratt, Director of HR & DM and founder of National Bullying Helpline

The term Gaslighting is a 'label' which embraces a cocktail of inappropriate and often manipulative workplace practices. Sadly, these unacceptable practices are commonplace. Historically, we have described these practices as 'subtle workplace bullying'.

The term Gaslighting is based on a 1944 film 'Gaslight' starring Ingrid Bergman. Bergman's character marries and mysterious things start to happen to her in her marriage. Her husband convinces her that she is imaging things, when in fact he is scheming with criminal intent.

Psychologists describe Gaslighting as a subtle but unhealthy manipulative behaviour.

An employee who is the subject of Gaslighting will likely, certainly initially, struggle to understand what is occurring – similar to Bergman's character in the film.

Typically, an employee cannot 'put their finger on the problem'. They believe they are imagining things. They may even feel 'non-credible'. All the employee knows is they feel constantly undermined or excluded and they start to develop trust issues within the workplace. Their confidence and productivity levels suffer. They start to feel unwell.

They may even be signed off work by their GP with work-related stress.

Gaslighting is classic abuse of power. It is bullying. It's a manipulate power-game, which individuals or groups of individuals play within a workplace with deliberate intent to control an individual or control a situation. A perpetrator could be a co-worker or a line manager. However, Gaslighting may be cultural ie: from the top down, condoned at Corporate management level. It's an entirely unacceptable, subtle, management style.

What are the signs of Gaslighting?

Spotting the signs of Gaslighting is easier than you might think. Signs (not exclusively) include:

♦ A lack of openness and transparency. This may be with immediate line management in a one-on-one relationship or it may be at Corporate level involving an entire Executive Board and/or a business owner.

♦ A reluctance to minute meetings or draw-up file-notes. We should not assume this is down to a lack of management skills. It could be intentional and therefore far more serious.

♦ Refusal to follow policies unless it suits the business. For example, reluctance to acknowledge a verbal employee complaint or investigate a formal grievance but at the same time applying a forceful approach to performance management and disciplinary policies.

♦ Drip-feeding information or failing to provide full facts (which we have historically described as 'setting a person up to fail') or repeatedly re-scheduling meetings or withholding important information.

♦ Moving goal-posts or changing elements of an employee job description without first engaging in discussion or making reference to a change-management policy.

♦ Springing surprises ie: calling last-minute meetings but failing to share data or advise in advance what the purpose of the meeting is and what the likely outcomes may be.

♦ Knee-jerk suspensions over minor issues where a discussion or an informal meeting will have resolved any misunderstanding.

♦ Instant dismissals without following due process.

♦ The inappropriate use of the term 'Redundancy' simply because a management team want to release an employee and/or make changes within the business.

♦ Failure to carry out fair and thorough grievance or disciplinary investigations and deciding in advance of an investigation that an employee's complaint will not be upheld (ie: pre-determined outcomes). Warning signs include a refusal to appoint an independent, impartial, workplace investigator in grievance and disciplinary cases.

♦ Undermining behaviour intended to destroy an employee's confidence. For example, open criticism or alleging that others have complained where, in fact, there is no evidence of any complaint.

Is Gaslighting affecting you at work?

It is highly likely in your workplace at some point in time. You may know someone who has experienced this behaviour. You may be experiencing Gaslighting yourself at this moment in time.

The above are just a few examples. It really can be, and often is, extremely deep-rooted within business, whether that business is private or public sector. It is important to remember that any one of the above circumstances, in isolation, does not necessarily make a case for Gaslighting. However, where a number of the above scenarios are occurring at work, and you are anxious, seek help immediately.

I was bullied out of my job. Lockdown is a chance to end toxic work culture

What does it say about our creative industry that so many people have a story of being bullied in the workplace?

By Sue Higgs, advertising creative director, writing in *Campaign* magazine

I've been in this industry for many years and for much of that time I've harboured a secret. I recently posted an article on LinkedIn in which I shared my very personal, traumatic experience.

I was bullied out of my job at a big agency nearly a decade ago by a man in a senior position there. Before leaving my job, I was close to having a breakdown. Even though I complained about his abusive behaviour and asked for help, nothing was done and he continued to work at the agency for many years after I left.

While I was working with this person, I was systematically broken down, sidelined and made to feel worthless. Every day, he would ask me why I bothered coming into work and told the account people that I was useless and warned them not to work with me.

I wasn't the only one he bullied. HR had a huge dossier of complaints about him, but they told me they could do nothing because he was too senior and had won awards. The stress took a major toll on both my mental and physical health. But I had to stick it out for as long as possible, because I was a single mum with three kids depending on me. I needed the job. I had no choice but to put up with the abuse.

At the time, a person in HR advised me to document the bullying in a diary. It makes me very sad to read that diary now. Even though I'm not going through that horrible experience any more, I still bear the scars. I was a very confident person before this happened. I'm less self-assured now and I find I question myself much more.

The Covid-19 confinement has encouraged a lot of introspection, and with the Black Lives Matter protests going on and all the inequalities and injustices being exposed round the world right now, I felt inspired to call out this unacceptable behaviour that still goes on unquestioned in many places of work.

After I published my LinkedIn post, I was shocked by the huge number of people who responded saying that they had similar experiences at work. So many people in advertising messaged me with their stories – brutal, raw tales of lives destroyed, mental health issues, anxiety and self-doubt. I had messages from many women, but also a surprisingly large number of men too. Everyone had one thing in common: their lives had been made a misery by someone in power and it was all hushed up. The more I read, the more I realised just how vast the problem is and how it's seen as some accepted norm.

But what does this say about the industry we work in?

Our entire value system is wrong. If we are not holding people in power to account simply because they have plaudits or influence, then we have created a seriously toxic culture.

How can an industry that cites creativity as its currency sanction such brutal behaviour?

Telling my story has felt liberating and cathartic. And my current employers have been incredibly supportive. But what I really want is an end to the system in this industry that enables bullying.

HR needs to be a safe space for people, but it also needs complete independence from senior management and the ability to take decisive action against those who abuse power, regardless of who they are. We need to call out this abuse for what it is. Now that I've found my voice, I won't be silenced and I won't stop until this behaviour is curbed.

This issue is even more critical now that there is such economic uncertainty ahead. People will be more afraid of speaking up in case they lose their jobs and their livelihoods. The onus should not be on the victims to fight their corner. It is the responsibility of the powers that be at every agency to ensure there is zero tolerance of abuse at all levels in an organisation.

The lockdown has given us a chance to reflect on our lives and what we want to take forward into the future. We could be using this as an opportunity to eradicate a toxic behaviour that has long been ingrained in the DNA of our industry. Let's start putting the value on the leaders and colleagues who raise the people around them up, not those who grind them down.

Sue Higgs is group creative director at Grey

29 June 2020

How to recognise when you're being bullied at work and what to do about it

In his latest blog, Dr Chris Tiplady explores the subject of bullying and the many different ways of responding to and resolving aggressive or intimidating behaviour.

By Dr Chris Tiplady

I have been bullied before – have we all at some point?

Maybe it happened to you as a child or more recently, but the bullying that affects us as adults is different to that which happens in the playground. It is not always easy to detect – there may just be a niggling uncertainty at the back of your mind that something isn't quite right, rather than noisy shows of aggression and intimidation.

I'm lucky enough not to have experienced a great deal first hand, but I've witnessed it countless times. I particularly remember the questioning conversation I had with two medical students about an experience in an out-patient clinic they were meant to attend.

In an effort to introduce themselves to the consultant whose appointments they were supposed to be observing, they gently knocked on the door of the consulting room, and after a brief exchange, were told in no uncertain terms to go back out and wait until called. They eventually went back in and were told to sit in the corner and stay quiet: they were not to speak unless spoken to. They had an hour of angry questioning in front of and in between patients which left them feeling shaken and confused.

I also remember the doctor who felt they would never be able to go into their chosen specialty as they had disagreed with a consultant, who'd proceeded to shout at them across a ward of patients. A terrible thought – that one incidence could be enough to make some rethink their career.

Not only do these attacks hurt those who they're directed at: research has shown that witnessing bullying and harassment has a significant impact on the health and well-being of bystanders. Bystanders, of course, includes patients.

It is really hard for me to share stories like this, since every single one is upsetting. But I don't want to shirk from sharing examples – I just hope one day I stop hearing about them altogether.

Of course, the only way that will ever happen is if we can all recognise bullying, know what to do when it happens and have someone willing to sort it out. In this blog, I'll explore how to recognise bullying and what can you do when you find yourself in situations like these.

In the moment

Keep calm

No matter if someone's behaviour is outright aggressive or subtly undermining, try to stay as calm as you can when it's happening. It's deeply unpleasant to feel attacked, but don't escalate things into a fight. Also, try not to make apologies for yourself – feeling like you have to apologise is one of those alarm bells that you are being bullied and helps to validate the other person's nasty behaviour.

Reflect and clarify

Reflection is a useful tactic to unearth what's really going on with someone: acknowledge what is happening and being said, and repeat phrases back for confirmation. If you feel safe to, you can ask them to explain why they are saying or doing things. I think of this as my "customer services mode".

After the incident

Take some time to process what happened

Step back. Recognise your feelings in the heat of the moment. Sometimes after a bit of time reflecting, you may realise that what upset you was a bit of hard truth: a lot of people have mistaken well-meaning, direct feedback for harsh criticism.

Similarly, you might realise that this person really overstepped the mark, making you feel belittled or humiliated. Some warning signs include:

- disbelief and shock at someone's behaviour, that stays with you even after you have got home and calmed down

- dread and worry about meeting this person again

- an unexplainable feeling of shame, even though you have done nothing wrong

- a feeling like you were powerless to say or do anything to resolve the conflict

- a feeling like you are being made to apologise

- the urge to go and tell someone what just happened.

If that's the case…

Talk to someone

It doesn't matter who – it just has to be someone you trust. They may be your supervisor, your line manager, a colleague, a friend or one of the more official roles that many places have – like a Freedom to Speak up Guardian, the Director of Medical Education or a College Representative.

This person needs to have the skills to listen and help you define what's happened. The right person may also be aware of other concerns about the individual.

Write it all down

Where were you, what day, what time, what else was happening, who was around, who saw or heard things? You forget this kind of detail very rapidly and it can all be very useful in the future. Keep emails or any correspondence you get from the person causing you upset.

Remember that emails are an easy way of escalating conflicts as well – they are the road rage of communications. Avoid replying if you're feeling angry. I used to have an inbox

folder labelled "emails that made me angry". Just putting them there was helpful.

Taking it further

So – you've sought support and processed your experience and things are not resolved. At this point, you have a few options.

Speak to the person in question

Maybe on reflection you've realised that what happened was unintentional – despite its impact – and the person just doesn't realise how it made you feel. This is a situation where talking to the person directly can help.

You need to prepare that chat and plan it through so you know exactly what you want to get across. Be objective: say in a factual way what happened and why it was unacceptable.

You may want to do this with a friend and practise what you want to say. You may even want that friend to come with you when you talk.

Use a mediator

Resolution of the situation could also be achieved by a manager, a good friend or a skilled mediator. Many organisations now have access to mediation as it is a very effective alternative to the more formal processes.

Mediation is useful when a relationship at work has deteriorated to the point that angry words are being exchanged and behaviours simply fan the flames of conflict. Mediators are non-judgmental and will, through a series of conversations, listen to both sides of the story attempting to understand what has led to the current situation. They will help people understand their feelings and actions and most importantly explore what will resolve a dispute. Many people who have been through conflict just want it to stop and to return to a nice (or even just civil) working relationship. If this is what you are after then mediation is ideal.

Make a formal complaint

If informal routes of resolution don't result in the outcome you want, you can make a formal complaint. Every organisation will have a policy for doing this, but it needs careful consideration: once formal policies are triggered, things can become very unpleasant for everyone, with statements, investigations and lots of emotions flying around.

Importantly, that doesn't mean it isn't sometimes exactly the right thing to do. Those who bully and harass shouldn't be able to do so with impunity. Formal processes are there to empower those who are victimised – as well as making sure genuinely unpleasant and disruptive people aren't allowed to continue hurting others.

Final thoughts

When it comes to dealing with bullying and harassment, many people are unsure what to do or how far to take things. I always ask people what they want to achieve. If you simply want the person to apologise, that's a very different route to if you want them formally punished.

Personally, I am lucky not to encounter this too often, partly as I make sure I am very clear that any behaviour that makes people feel uncomfortable is completely unacceptable. We can all afford to cultivate more awareness of the impact that our behaviours and words have on those around us and must all play a part in calling out any behaviour that could be perceived as bullying or undermining. A safe and nastiness-free working environment is our collective responsibility and it will always make care better for our patients.

24 April 2019

We need to look further than Priti Patel, bullying in Parliament is rife

Another day has passed and more allegations of bullying by the Home Secretary Priti Patel have surfaced.

And yet, somehow, she clings on to her role – thanks in no small part to the backing she has received from the prime minister. She has denied any wrongdoing and her supporters say it is a 'smear campaign', but it is difficult to imagine a leader in any other walk of life being allowed to stay in a position of power when they are facing such claims.

But this is not an article about Patel. Or at least, not about her specifically. It is a call for us to use this moment to examine not only the finer points of her alleged behaviour – as important as that will be to the case against her – but also the structural problems in our politics that allow bullies (and there are many, even if the claims against Patel are not upheld) to thrive. Compassion in Politics, a cross-party organisation, has spoken to civil servants about the Patel case and it's clear hers is an unusual one – but not in the sense that you might imagine. What is unusual is that someone as senior as Philip Putnam chose to speak out against her. More junior servants have told us that bullying by ministers is not uncommon. One said that they consider a meeting with a minister to have gone well if they were not shouted at or verbally abused. A fact universally acknowledged within the civil service – that some ministers are frequent bullies – is now being widely discussed outside it. That is why we must use this moment to embed structural reform.

Push and pull factors combine to allow bullies to succeed in politics. The system pulls bullies to the top – or rather, holds back those of a more socially-orientated, sensitive disposition. The whipping system is formalised bullying. The two-party system forces politicians to see members of other parties as opponents in a war, rather than equal participants in the policy-making process. Parliamentary debates are raucous, rough, and rowdy: many personality types will simply not be able to flourish or contribute meaningfully in such conditions. And these are just the systems that a backbench MP has to tolerate – imagine the psychological profile of the kind of person who rises through that baptism of fire to lead the country.

Then there are the push factors that prevent a civil servant from speaking out. One of the civil servants that we spoke to regarding the Patel case said they were not at all surprised that the Home Office claimed no official complaints had been received regarding the secretary of state's behaviour. They even implied it was rather disingenuous of the Home Office to make such a statement since, in their experience, most departments do not have any formal, independent procedure for a civil servant to complain about their ministerial masters. Ministers are subject to an entirely different set of rules created arbitrarily by the prime minister and their chief of staff. There are other cultural factors that might inhibit a civil servant from speaking out. Some of these are similar to those raised brilliantly by Gemma White QC in her report into bullying in Parliament (note the difference here – White looked at the experience of staff employed directly by MPs as opposed to civil servants who work for the government). She found that many staffers were afraid of speaking out against an MP for fear that it would tarnish their future career or they would be perceived as acting with disloyalty to the party apparatus. The same must surely be true for a civil service, which prides itself on the work it performs for the government. Indeed, the civil service code requires that employees 'act in a way which deserves and retains the confidence of ministers'.

That a troubled system will continue to operate without reform whether Patel stays or goes is the clear and present danger. And that's also why those of us invested in a more compassionate, cooperative, and inclusive form of politics have to act now to build that alternative vision. This week the new All Party Group for Compassionate Politics launched in Parliament with parliamentarians from six parties. This group will now provide a vehicle for reform and start creating a proper complaints process inside the government so that civil servants can, if necessary, anonymously complain about their treatment at the hands of ministers.

16 March 2020

Can you unintentionally bully someone? Here's the science

An article from The Conversation.

By Geoff Beattie

THE CONVERSATION

I was nine. Some girl, maybe around 15 or 16, old enough to tower over me, asked whether Bill Beattie was my brother. I nodded. Without saying another word she grabbed me by my hair and started to drag me across the street – pulling out clumps of it. The whole time she was swearing about my brother – how he thought he was too good for her. I was bent double, trotting to keep up with her in her rage. In shock, I prayed that nobody had witnessed the attack.

I never mentioned this to anyone – it was too humiliating. I always saw it as a particularly nasty act of bullying, but now I'm not so sure. Bullying, it seems, can be a slippery concept. Fast forward half a century and Priti Patel, the UK's home secretary, has managed to keep her job, despite reports of bullying – claiming she didn't mean to upset anyone. So what actually counts as bullying?

According to the psychologist Dan Olweus from the University of Bergen in Norway, a pioneer of bullying research, a person is bullied "when he or she is exposed, repeatedly and over time, to negative actions". Such action requires that someone "intentionally inflicts, or attempts to inflict, injury or discomfort upon another". Others have added that a power imbalance is a third important criterion – the most popular guy in class, for example, has power in the form of backup when needed.

But several studies have shown that children tend to equate bullying with direct physical aggression. Tracy Vaillancourt from the University of Ottawa in Canada examined children and young people's definitions of bullying and found that they rarely included the three prominent criteria - only 1.7% mentioned intentionality, 6% repetition and 26% power imbalance. Almost all participants (92%) emphasised aggressive behaviours as bullying, even one-off occurrences.

What's more, the definition seems to get both Patel and my attacker off the hook – at least at first glance. In my case, although there was a power imbalance, the assault was never repeated, even though the girl continued to give me dirty looks that made me uncomfortable. But fleeting facial expressions are nebulous and vague, always difficult to interpret. And perhaps my assailant didn't even intend the humiliation or see a power imbalance. I was a boy after all, living in the highly sexist times of Belfast in the sixties. Boys were meant to be stronger than girls.

The event still gave me sleepless nights, bad dreams and this odd psychosomatic tenderness in my scalp – to this day, I occasionally catch myself massaging it. If you want to understand bullying, assessing the psychological effects on the victim is paramount.

When it comes to Patel, Sir Alex Allan, the prime minister's ethics adviser, said: "Her approach on occasions has amounted to … bullying in terms of the impact felt by individuals." He added Patel's behaviour met the civil service definition of bullying as "intimidating or insulting behaviour

that makes an individual feel uncomfortable, frightened, less respected or put down".

Allan noted instances of shouting and swearing, and found that Patel had breached the ministerial code, but perhaps "unintentionally".

The wider situation

So does that mean it's always a bully's word against the victim's – intent versus psychological damage? Not really. By scrutinising actual behaviour, looking for evidence of intention and assessing the wider situation, we can get further clues.

Take intent. People can obviously lie about their intentions. And just because someone doesn't have a conscious, calculated agenda of bullying another person, they can still, perhaps subconsciously, intend to harm them in isolated and emotional moments. They may act out because they feel attacked, thinking their outbursts are a form of self-defence rather than aggression – failing to see how much power they actually have. Or they may think their behaviour is a form of "tough love", boosting achievement in the victim. But that doesn't necessarily make them innocent.

People accused of bullying in the workplace tend to understand their behaviour mainly in terms of the situation – their attention is on the pressures of the job. They are trying to "get the job done" in a difficult and stressed environment, raising their voice if need be.

But those around the perpetrator, the observers, are able to see the behaviour of the person more clearly and, on occasion, can infer stable characteristics about them across time and place. Interestingly, the former Home Office permanent secretary Sir David Normington has claimed that Patel possibly bullied staff in three departments and not just the Home Office. Observers are also able to sense the anticipatory fear and dread caused by the behaviour.

As psychologist Heinz Leymann from the University of Stockholm noted in 1990, many of the behaviours involved in bullying may be fairly common in everyday life but they can, nevertheless, cause considerable harm and humiliation. Generally when it comes to bullying, it may not be the behaviour itself that makes the victim suffer – it is the frequency of the act and other situational factors relating to power differences or inescapable interactions that may cause the anxiety, misery and suffering.

Government ministers have tremendous amounts of power. And home secretaries of all people must be able to take other people's perspective. They need to be able to read anxiety, misery and suffering. How else can they draw up effective policies involving all of us? That nameless girl in Belfast, however, can perhaps be excused.

23 November 2020

Key Facts

- The Equality Act 2010 identifies nine 'protected characteristics' and children and young people can have or be perceived to have more than one 'protected characteristic' and as a result may be bullied because of a number of prejudices. (page 1)

- 47% of people aged 12-18 believed they were bullied because of their appearance. (page 7)

- 44% of people aged 12-18 said being bullied left them feeling anxious. (page 8)

- 67% of people aged 12-18 didn't think they deserved to be bullied, 10% did think they deserved to be bullied and 23% were unsure. (page 8)

- 64% of people aged 12-18 who were bullied said they tried to ignore it. (page 9)

- 12% of people aged 12-18 said they had changed or hidden a part if who they are in order to avoid getting bullied. (page 9)

- Around one in five children aged 10 to 15 years in England and Wales (19%) experienced at least one type of online bullying behaviour in the year ending March 2020, equivalent to 764,000 children. (page 10)

- In the year ending March 2020, 7 out of 10 (70%) children aged 10 to 15 years who experienced an online bullying behaviour said this was by someone from their school. (page 11)

- For the year ending March 2020, 22% of children aged 10 to 15 years who had experienced a type of online bullying behaviour said that they were emotionally affected a lot by these incidents. (page 12)

- Being called names, sworn at and insulted was the most frequently experience online bullying behaviour. (page 12)

- The most common reason for not reporting experiences of online bullying behaviours to anyone was that the victim did not think it was important. (page 13)

- In a recent study, data showed that those who bully are far more likely than average to have experienced a stressful or traumatic situation in the past 5 years. (page 17)

- 66% of the people who had admitted to bullying somebody else were male. (page 17)

- 1 in 3 of those who bully people daily told us that they feel like their parents/guardians don't have enough time to spend with them. They are more likely to come from larger families and are more likely to live with people other than their biological parents. (page 17)

- The first researcher to investigate bullying – in Norway – used the word "mobbing" to describe it in 1973. Most Western countries have borrowed the English term for bullying, yet this is not always the case. (page 18)

- In 2017, the Workplace Bullying Institute estimated that 60.3m workers in the US alone have been affected by workplace bullying. (page 18)

- 27 per cent of children across the UK said bullying or someone being unkind to them was what worried them the most when using the internet. (page 21)

- A survey found that while 92 per cent of parents felt they knew how to advise their child on staying safe online, less than half (42 per cent) had agreed guidelines on what they do when using the internet. (page 21)

- A recent Ofcom report suggests that cyberbullying is not more of a widespread problem than real-life bullying. The report found that older children aged 12-15 are just as likely to experience "real life" bullying as bullying on social media. Younger children aged eight to 11 were found to be more likely to experience traditional bullying (14%) than online bullying (8%). (page 24)

- An international study by scientists in Britain, China and the US looked at data from 220,000 adolescents aged between 12 and 15 from 83 countries. It found more than one in eight youngsters across the world had suicidal behaviours, with bullying strongly associated to suicide attempts. (page 28)

- A TUC survey of its safety representatives last year found that they regarded bullying as the second biggest workplace issue after stress. They reported it to be worst in local and central government (cited by, respectively, 80 per cent and 71 per cent of respondents). (page 29)

- A survey of 4,200 people working in British science labs found that 43 per cent had been personally bullied, while 61 per cent had witnessed workplace bullying. (page 30)

- According to research by Employment law specialists Kew Law, the most commonly identified form of bullying in the workplace was overloading individuals with work. (page 31)

- The figures also show a general decrease in the likelihood of bullying as age increases – with only 23 per cent of 45-54 year olds saying they have experienced bullying, compared with 44 per cent of 21-24 year olds. (page 31)

- In addition, 40 per cent of female respondents said they had been bullied, compared with 31 per cent of male respondents. (page 31)

- Up to 46 per cent of employees surveyed said they would not report bullying behaviour with either the HR department or senior management, and 33 per cent would rather take it up with the bully directly than raise it with HR. (page 32)

Baiting

A method of provocation. To intentionally make someone angry by doing or saying things to annoy them.

Banter

An exchange of teasing remarks.

Bullying

A form of aggressive behaviour used to intimidate and someone. I can be inflicted physically and mentally (psychologically).

Cyberbullying

Cyberbullying is when technology is used to harass, embarass or threaten to hurt someone. A lot is done through social networking sites such as Facebook, Instagram and Twitter or via texts from mobile phones. With the use of technology on the rise, there are more and more incidents of cyberbullying.

Discrimination

Unfair treament against someone because of the group/class they belong to.

Harassment

Usually persistent (but not always), a behaviour that is intended to cause distress and offence. It can occur on the school playground, in the workplace or even at home.

Non-verbal abuse

Can be thought of as a kind of 'psychological warfare' because instead of using spoken words or direct physical violent behaviour, this form of abuse involves the use of mimicry (teasing someone by mimicking them), offensive gestures or body language.

Racist bullying

Targeting a person because of their race, colour or beliefs. There is a difference between racism and racial harassment: racial harassment refers to words and actions that are intentionally said/done to make the target feel small and degraded due to their race or ethnicity.

Self-harm/self-injury

Self-harm is the act of deliberately injuring or mutilating oneself. People injure themselves in many different ways, including cutting, burning, poisoning or hitting parts of their body. Self-harmers often see harming as a coping strategy and give a variety of motivations for hurting themselves including relieving stress or anxiety, focusing emotional pain and as a way of feeling in control. Although prevalent in young people it is not usually an attempt at suicide, although people who self-harm are statistcally more llkely to take their own lives than those who don't.

Sexual bullying

This includes a range of behaviours such as sexualised name calling and verbal abuse, mocking someone's sexual performance, ridiculing physical appearance, criticising sexual behaviour, spreading rumours about someone's sexuality or about sexual experiences they have had or not had, unwanted touching and physical assault. Sexual bullying is behaviour that is repeated over time and intends to victimise someone by using their gender, sexuality or sexual (in)experience to hurt them.

Social media

Media which are designed specifically for electronic communication. 'Social networking' websites allow users to interact using instant messaging, share information, photos and videos, and ultimately create an online community. Examples include Instagram, Snapchat, Twitter and WhatsApp.

Trolling

Trolling is when someone intentionally posts something online to provoke a reaction. The idea behind the trolling phenomenon is that it is about humour, mischief, and some argue, freedom of speech; it can be anything from a cheeky remark to a violent threat. However, sometimes these internet pranks can be taken too far, such as a person who defaces an internet tribute site, causing the victim's family further grief.

Verbal abuse

Words spoken out loud to cause harm, such as suggestive remarks, jokes or name-calling.

Activities

Brainstorming

♦ In small groups, discuss what you know about bullying:

- What kinds of bullying are there?

- Give some examples of bullying behaviour.

- Why do you think some people bully and some people are bullied?

- Give some examples of the effects of bullying.

Research

♦ Create an anonymous questionnaire that will be distributed among your class or year group to find out how many people have experience of bullying. Decide whether you want to focus on people who have been bullied or people who are bullies. Work in pairs to construct at least ten questions. Distribute your questionnaire, thinking carefully about how it will be returned anonymously, then gather your results and create a presentation for your class, including graphs and infographics if appropriate.

♦ With a partner, take a look at your school or college's anti-bullying policy. Discuss how effective you think it is. Are there any additions you would make? Write up any suggested amendments to the policy you and your partner have talked about and share with the rest of the class.

♦ Talk to friends and family who are in employment about their experiences of bullying in the workplace. Have they witnessed or experienced it? How was the situation dealt with? What are the differences between school bullies and work bullies? Write some notes and then feed back to your class.

♦ Read the article *We need to look further than Priti Patel, bullying in Parliament is rife* on pages 37-38 then go online and research other reports or incidents of bullying involving high-profile people or organisations. Write a summary of what you have found and how the situation was dealt with in some or all of the cases.

♦ Use the internet to research anti-bullying campaigns. Choose one you think sends a particularly strong and effective message. Discuss your reasons for choosing it with a classmate.

Design

♦ Choose one of the articles from this book and create an illustration to highlight the key themes of the piece.

♦ In small groups, design a school-based campaign that focuses on the effects of bullying. Choose one particular type of bullying for your campaign – cyberbullying, emotional, verbal or physical. You could use posters, articles in your school magazine or posts on your school social media channels.

♦ Design a horizontal banner that could be displayed as an advert on websites to highlight the effects of cyberbullying. Write a list of possible websites you think would be the most suitable to display the banner and would have the biggest impact.

♦ Create a meme with an anti-bullying message.

Oral

♦ In pairs, discuss the definitions of :

- Gaslighting

- Baiting

- Trolling

- Exclusion

♦ As a class, write down bullying scenarios on small pieces of paper (anonymously), fold them up and put them in a jar. Select a scenario at random, read it aloud or roleplay the situation and then discuss appropriate ways to deal with each one.

♦ In pairs, discuss why some types of bullying might be considered more serious than others.

♦ Go through this book and discuss the illustrations you come across. Think about what the artists are trying to portray in each piece.

♦ Speak to an adult you know about their experiences of childhood bullying. Ask them about how it affected them in the long term, whether they were a victim, perpetrator or bystander.

Reading/writing

♦ Imagine that you represent an anti-bullying charity/ organisation and compose a selection of social media posts for Twitter, Facebook and Instagram. The posts should act as a series of hard-hitting messages which inform people about the impact of bullying and the consequences for those who bully. You may also post links to external websites, videos and photos which provide further information if you think this is helpful.

♦ Write a list of the reasons why some types of bullying are harder to tackle than others.

♦ Imagine you have bullied someone and now you are remorseful and regret the suffering you have caused. Write a letter of apology to your victim explaining why you did it and why you are sorry.

♦ Write a paragraph about the impact of bullying on mental health.

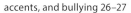

Acknowledgements

The publisher is grateful for permission to reproduce the material in this book. While every care has been taken to trace and acknowledge copyright, the publisher tenders its apology for any accidental infringement or where copyright has proved untraceable. The publisher would be pleased to come to a suitable arrangement in any such case with the rightful owner.

The material reproduced in ISSUES books is provided as an educational resource only. The views, opinions and information contained within reprinted material in ISSUES books do not necessarily represent those of Independence Educational Publishers and its employees.

Images

Cover image courtesy of iStock. All other images courtesy of Pixabay and Unsplash.

Illustrations

Simon Kneebone: pages 5, 23 & 36. Angelo Madrid: pages 3, 17 & 33.

Additional acknowledgements

With thanks to the Independence team: Shelley Baldry, Danielle Lobban, Jackie Staines and Jan Sunderland.

Tracy Biram

Cambridge, January 2021

About About Bullying

Recent studies show one in two people have experienced some form of bullying behaviour at some point in their life. Online bullying in particular has increased due to wider access to the internet and greater use of smartphones, social media and networking apps. This book looks at the latest UK statistics around bullying, its impact on victims and its prevalence in schools and workplaces alike.

About issues

issues is a unique series of cross-curricular resource books for key stage 3, 4 & above. The series explores contemporary social issues, stimulating debate among readers of all levels. Each book presents a range of facts and opinions, providing the reader with an unbiased overview of the topic.

Titles contain articles and statistics from all key players involved in the topic covered, and include a range of diverse opinions. Elements include:

- Key facts
- Magazine features
- Charity group literature
- Cartoons and illustrations
- Journal and book extracts
- Extracts from government reports
- Statistics, including tables and graphs
- Newspaper reports and feature articles
- Accessible, easy to photocopy, full colour layouts
- Glossaries, time-lines and diagrams

independence
educational publishers

issues online
resources for schools, colleges & libraries

RRP:

Orders can be placed directly with the publisher:

Independence, The Studio, High Green, Great Shelford, Cambridge, CB22 5EG, England

Fax: 01223 550806
Phone: 01223 550801
Email: issues@independence.co.uk

www.independence.co.uk
www.issuesonline.co.uk